THE
LITTLE
BOOK
OF
SOMERSET

MAURICE FELLS

The History Press

First published 2018

The History Press
The Mill, Brimscombe Port
Stroud, Gloucestershire, GL5 2QG
www.thehistorypress.co.uk

British Library Cataloguing in Publication Data.
A catalogue record for this book is available from the British Library.

ISBN 978 0 7509 8799 8

Typesetting and origination by The History Press
Printed and bound in Great Britain by TJ International Ltd

CONTENTS

INTRODUCTION

Somerset is a remarkable county. It is a place where history, mystery, myths and legends abound. It also has a rich literary heritage evocative of 'Old England'. The Romantic poets William Wordsworth and Samuel Taylor Coleridge lived for a while in Nether Stowey, Alfoxden and Porlock. It is said that while walking the coastal paths in west Somerset they were inspired to write some of their best-known poetry. There is a part of Exmoor that will always be known as 'Lorna Doone' country after the book of that name written by R.D. Blackmore. Meanwhile, Jane Austen lived in Bath for five years and set much of her work in the city. Bath also inspired Mary Shelley to complete her great work, *Frankenstein*. Then there was the writer Evelyn Waugh, who spent the last years of his life in Combe Florey. Such was his love for Somerset that the American poet T.S. Eliot not only immortalised the village of East Coker in one of his poems but also left instructions for his ashes to be interred in the local church.

Many of the myths and legends are focused around the Somerset Levels. Did Joseph of Arithamea bury the Holy Grail at Glastonbury? Are King Arthur and his queen buried here and did King Alfred the Great really burn the cakes at nearby Athelney? True or false, the stories have helped to build Somerset's most unusual character.

Somerset is also a county of marshland, ancient towns and villages, seaside resorts, historic caves, Roman baths and verdant rolling hills. An early twentieth-century lyricist was so inspired by the hills that he wrote a song about them. Somerset is, of course, the home of Cheddar cheese and cider. The latter, originally produced in small sheds on farms all over the county, was once given to farm labourers as part of their wages. Today, cider-making has become a state-of-the-art multi-million pound industry, with one farm in the county sending out some 4 million pints a year to pubs, clubs and supermarkets all over the country. Perhaps sales were boosted by Adge Cutler and the Wurzels, who introduced the nation to their 'Scrumpy and Western' style of music. One of their records, 'I Am a Cider Drinker', made the number three spot in the record charts.

But where does Somerset begin and end? Over the years there have been changes to the county's boundaries, none of which have pleased the locals. People living here have fierce local pride about their traditional and historic county. Indeed, there were massive protests in the 1970s when parts of it were transferred by central government into a newly formed county with the unoriginal and uninspiring name of Avon. There were more boundary changes twenty years later when Avon was abolished and the area was split into new unitary authorities. All these changes make the distinction between historic and administrative divisions even more confusing. Many people still talk of 'old Somerset' as their traditional home. For the purposes of this book I have joined them. *The Little Book of Somerset* takes in the magnificent spa city of Bath in the east, goes down to Exmoor in the west, across to Chard, the most southerly town in the county, and up to Portishead, its most northerly point sitting on the edge of the Severn Estuary. This is what the civil servants call the 'ceremonial county'.

Such a vast area has produced many heroes and heroines who have left us a variety of legacies. Turn these pages and you will find a truly extraordinary explorer, a creator of artificial limbs and a really enterprising entrepreneur who turned a military camp into the first of a national chain of holiday centres. Alongside their stories are many fascinating, maybe frivolous and sometimes bizarre facts. For example, if you don't know what egg shackling is then this book will tell you.

However, *The Little Book of Somerset* does not set out to be a dusty academic tome or a definitive or chronological history of the county. I have left others to do that. This is simply a compendium of interesting facts from both the past and present. I hope that they will interest newcomers to the county, holidaymakers and even those born and bred in Somerset who thought they really knew their county.

ACKNOWLEDGEMENTS

To put this book together I trawled through a variety of sources. I started by searching through my own archive of press releases, house magazines, pamphlets and other publicity material issued by old established firms and organisations of long ago, some now defunct. I accumulated this material through working as a journalist for West Country radio, television stations and newspapers. In the course of my work, I have met some of the people who appear on the following pages while researching them or the organisations with which they are closely connected. The librarians working in the reference sections of local public libraries have been extremely helpful, too. Local knowledge and my curiosity about anything West Country has also played a big part in putting together this book.

Various people have suggested ideas that were worth following up and I wish to thank them for their help. One of them was a good friend, Nigel Dando, who was once a district reporter in Frome for an evening newspaper and was most helpful in sharing with me his knowledge of the area and its people. I am greatly indebted to Janet and Trevor Naylor for their many helpful suggestions, especially regarding natural history. It is fair to say that without their help there could be big gaps in this book. However, any mistakes are mine, for which I apologise.

My thanks must also go to Nicola Guy at the History Press for asking me if I would like to write this title, and to the team who designed and laid out the following pages to make it such an attractive book.

ABOUT THE AUTHOR

Maurice Fells has long had a passionate interest in the history of the West Country, especially that of his native Bristol. He loves delving into old newspapers – some of them published well over 100 years ago – looking for any scrap of information about how our predecessors lived and worked, and their environment. He is a journalist by profession and has held key editorial posts in regional newspapers, radio and television newsrooms. Maurice is a familiar voice on BBC Radio Bristol talking about local history matters. In addition to this book he has written *Clifton History You Can See, The A-Z of Curious Bristol, The Little Book of Bristol* and *Bristol Plaques,* all published by The History Press.

WHAT THEY SAY ABOUT SOMERSET

Clevedon has the most character, the widest diversity of scenery, and the fewest really hideous buildings. It has been saved by being on the road to nowhere.

Sir John Betjeman, Poet Laureate from 1972–84

On the centenary of the town's pier, John Betjeman said: 'Long live Clevedon as a complete town, which it would not be if it ever lost its pier.'

The novelist and poet Sylvia Townsend Warner wrote: 'One cannot travel through Somerset without feeling that one is being handed on from one set of hills to another.'

After visiting the north Somerset village of Pill on horseback, John Wesley, founder of Methodism, wrote in his journal: 'I rode to Pill, a place famous from generation to generation for stupid, brutal, abandoned wickedness.'

In his book *A Tour Thro the Whole Island of Great Britain and Wales,* Daniel Defoe described Minehead as being 'the best port and safest harbour on this side of all these counties'. In Yeovil, Defoe noted the town's industry: 'This is a market town of good resort; and some clothing carried on or near it, but not much. Its main manufacture at this time is the making of gloves.'

Defoe described the villagers of Cheddar as 'cowkeepers' and went on to say that the local cheese was 'the best cheese that England affords, if not the whole world'.

In her book *Through England on a Side Saddle in the Time of William and Mary*, travel writer Celia Fiennes wrote of the Roman baths in Bath: 'The Ladies go into the bath with garments made of fine yellow canvas, which is stiff and made large with great sleeves like a parson's gown; the water fills it up so that it is borne off so that your shape be not seen.'

When the diarist Samuel Pepys visited the Roman baths he wrote: 'They are not so large as I expected, but yet pleasant; and the town most of stone and clean, though the streets generally narrow.'

In an autobiography that he called *Boy: Tales of Childhood*, the children's writer Roald Dahl, who went to school in Weston-super-Mare in 1925, described the town as a 'slightly seedy seaside resort'. Despite his unfavourable comment, the town unveiled a blue plaque in 2018 commemorating Dahl's time in Weston.

Robert Southey, who was Poet Laureate from 1813 until his death in 1843, wrote of Ashton: 'The beautiful vale of Ashton, the place of all others which I remember with most feeling.' His mother's family lived in Long Ashton for generations and some of his relations are buried in the churchyard.

The prolific American writer John Steinbeck regarded the time he spent in Somerset as some of the happiest days of his life. He wrote: 'Time loses all its meaning. The peace I have dreamed about is here, a real thing: thick as a stone and feelable and something for your hands.'

1

AROUND THE COUNTY

WHAT'S IN A NAME?

Quite a lot, it seems, if you live in Wincanton. Believe it or not this small town – its population is under 6,000 – in south Somerset is twinned with a place that does not exist. Its 'twinning' partner, Ankh Morpork, is a fictional city created by the author Sir Terry Pratchett in his comic fantasy Discworld series. Wincanton and Ankh Morpork have been twinned since 2002. The late Sir Terry had a close relationship with Wincanton and was in the town seven years later to unveil road names at a new housing development. His books had inspired the street names Peach Pie Street and Treacle Mine Road.

However, like many other towns and cities across the country, Wincanton is officially twinned with places that do exist on terra firma. It linked up in 1975 with the French towns Gennes and Les Rosiers. Then in 1991 another twinning arrangement was made – this time with the German town, Lahnau.

How Somerset May Have Got Its Name
In 658 the Saxons defeated the Romano–Celtic people and captured eastern Somerset. The Saxons gave it the name Summertun, and it seems to have been quite an important village. In 949 the Witan, a kind of parliament, met at Somerton. Around 1270 the county courts and the county jail moved there.

For a short time Somerton was the county town of Somerset. It's said that the county's name comes from the Anglo–Saxon Sumorsaete, meaning 'land of the summer people'. In the past people could only settle there in the summer as in winter the land was flooded.

The Curry Villages

Some villages have 'Curry' as part of their name, as in Curry Rivel, Curry Mallet and North Curry. However, this has nothing to do with the spicy meal. There are several theories as to its origin. One is that 'Curry' comes from the Celtic word 'crwy', meaning 'boundary'. Another explanation is that Curry is a corruption of St Cyrig, a pre-Saxon Celtic bishop.

Town's 'Royal' Name

The market town of Chard – the most southerly town in the county – takes its name from Cerdic, who was the first King of Wessex. Chard has its roots deeply buried in Saxon times and was the ancient capital of the kingdom of Wessex.

Somerset Overseas

There are thirty-six places in the world with the name Somerset. Twenty-three of them are in America. Other 'Somersets' can be found in Guyana, Jamaica, Australia, South Africa and Bermuda.

UNESCO Honour

Bath is one of the two cities in the county of Somerset. In 1987 it was inscribed by UNESCO as a World Heritage Site. It is unusual for an entire city to be given this honour. UNESCO says that such sites are 'places of outstanding universal value to the whole of humanity'. The phrase 'outstanding universal value' means cultural and/or natural significance. UNESCO added the city of Bath as a 'cultural site' to its list because of its Roman remains, eighteenth-century architecture, eighteenth-century town planning, its social setting, hot springs and landscape setting. Famous World Heritage Sites include the Taj Mahal, pyramids of Giza, the Great Wall of China and the Grand Canyon.

THE ROMANS WERE HERE

On the authority of the future emperor Vespasian, the Second Legion Augusta invaded Somerset from the south-east in AD 47. The county remained part of the Roman Empire until around AD 409, when the Roman occupation of Britain came to an end.

Natural thermal springs beneath the city of Bath produce 1,170,000 litres of hot spring water every day. Bath has been a spa destination since the Romans built their baths here in AD 70 using water from the springs. These are the only hot springs in Britain.

In April 2018 permission was given by Bath and North East Somerset Council for heat exchangers to be installed in the Roman Baths to convert heat from the underground springs into renewable energy. The energy recovered from the water will be used to provide under-floor heating for Bath Abbey and surrounding buildings.

The Romans had their own name for Bath, calling it Aquae Sulis – Aquae meaning water and Sulis being the name of the Goddess of the hot springs at Bath.

Bathing in the baths used to be a common sight but is no longer allowed. All the same, the Great Bath is regularly drained of its 250,000 litres of thermal waters so that a team of cleaners can remove sludge and algae from its Roman floor. When the Great Bath is full the water is just over 5ft deep.

A record number of 1,123,633 people visited the Roman Baths in the year 2016–17.

COUNTY ON THE MOVE

Large chunks of Somerset, including the whole of Bath, were taken out of the county on 1 April 1974 and put into a newly created county called Avon. Despite the date this was no April Fool's Day joke but part of local government boundary changes made by Whitehall. Avon became the county that people either loved or loathed, even before it officially came into existence. The protests were numerous. Letters to politicians, petitions signed by thousands of people and even specially written protest songs calling for the abolition of Avon made the headlines.

Twenty-two years later – also on 1 April – the county of Avon was abolished. In another major local government shake-up, Whitehall this time created what is known as the ceremonial county of Somerset. This consists of the district council areas of West Somerset, South Somerset, Taunton Deane, Mendip and Sedgemoor. Two new unitary authorities were also created – North Somerset, which takes in Weston-super-Mare and Clevedon, and Bath & North East Somerset, commonly referred to by the voters as BANES.

However, Avon is a name that refuses to die, even though the county was abolished in 1996. The name lives on in the titles of Avon and Somerset Police, Avon Coroner's Court, Avon Fire and Rescue Service, Avon Wildlife Trust and a host of other organisations.

A FLAG FOR SOMERSET

The Somerset flag depicts the traditional dragon emblem of the county. It has featured on the county council's coat of arms for more than 100 years. However, it is ultimately derived from the banners borne by Alfred the Great and his kinsmen during the Viking Wars, which were variously described as bearing red or gold dragons or wyverns. On the flag a red dragon appears against a yellow background.

TOPOGRAPHY

Somerset is sandwiched between Wiltshire to the east, Dorset to the south-east, and Devon to the south-west, while Bristol provides part of its northern boundary. The 40-mile coastline of the Bristol Channel and Severn Estuary also forms part of the north-west and south-west borders.

Somerset covers an area of 4,171 square kilometres; this makes it England's seventh biggest county by area.

The county is home to two cities – Bath and Wells – and more than 400 villages, including Beardly Batch, Beer Crocombe, Charlton Mackrell, Chedzoy, Clapton in Gordano, Compton Pauncefoot, Huish Episcopi, Keinton Mandeville, Nempnett Thrubwell, Queen Camel, Preston Plucknett and Vobster. There are also thirty small towns in the county.

At an altitude of 413ft, Wiveliscombe (in the south of the county) is the highest town in Somerset.

The last census in 2011 showed that the total population of the ceremonial county of Somerset was 948,900.

THE COUNTY TOWN

The south Somerset town of Somerton describes itself as the 'Ancient Royal Town of Wessex'. At one time it was the county town of Somerset but that status has been held by Taunton since 1336. Taunton is home to the administrative headquarters of the county council, which has fifty-five members and is based at County Hall. The town also hosts 40 Commando, Royal Marines; the United Kingdom Hydrographic Office; and the headquarters of Somerset County Cricket Club.

TOP TOWN

The town of Frome, with a population of about 30,000, is the best place in which to live in the south-west of England, according to the *Sunday Times* survey for 2018. Factors from jobs, schools and broadband speed to culture, community spirit and local shops were all taken into account. The judges said they also noted The Compassionate Frome plan, which was set up five years ago by a local doctor to help people cope with ill health. It has resulted in 17 per cent fewer hospital admissions in the area. Frome was one of the largest towns in Somerset until the Industrial Revolution, and was larger than Bath from AD 950 until 1650.

HISTORY YOU CAN SEE

Somerset has 523 ancient monuments, 192 conservation areas, 41 parks and gardens, 36 English Heritage sites and 19 National Trust sites.

The county has 11,500 buildings listed as being of architectural or historical interest. In west Somerset the village of Dunster alone has more than 200 Grade I, Grade II and Grade II* listed buildings. They range from Dunster Castle and Gatehouse to the seventeenth-century octagonal Yarn Market in the middle of the High Street and the stone cottages almost hidden away in the side streets of Dunster.

One of the most unusual listed buildings is at Langport, where a perpendicular building commonly called the Hanging Chapel – more formally known as the Chantry Chapel of the Blessed Virgin Mary – sits on top of a thirteenth-century archway across the road. It has Grade I listed status.

More than 10 million documents relating to the history of the county are archived at the Somerset Heritage Centre at Norton Fitzwarren, on the edge of Taunton. The oldest document dates back to AD 705 and is a contract signed by the Saxon King Ine. The original records office was part of Wells Cathedral.

The village of Wedmore on the Somerset Levels has written itself into the history books, being the place where in AD 878 Alfred the Great made peace with the Danes, followed by nearly a fortnight of feasting and ceremonies at his palace.

THE 'SECRET STONES'

Almost hidden away in the Chew Valley village of Stanton Drew is Somerset's answer to Wiltshire's Stonehenge. In a farmer's field is the third largest complex of prehistoric standing stones in the country after Stonehenge and Avebury in Wiltshire. At Stanton Drew there are three circles of massive stones in the field and what is called a three-stone 'cove' stands in the back garden of the Druids Arms pub just along the road. The largest circle has twenty-six upright stones, although English Heritage believes there may have been up to thirty. On average the stones are each about 9ft high.

Dating The Stones

An English Heritage survey of the site in 1997 showed that the stones were just a part of a more elaborate complex. Archaeologists found that lying under the largest circle, which they call the Great Circle, are the remains of a complex pattern of buried pits, arranged in nine concentric rings within the stone circle, and further pits at the centre. Stone circles like these are believed to date back to the Late Neolithic and Early Bronze Age (around 3000–2000 BC). Although the stones are on private land, they are managed by English Heritage. Compared with Stonehenge and Avebury, the stones of Stanton Drew get very few visitors, possibly because of their seclusion.

THE SYMBOL OF A TOWN CALLED STREET

The roadside sign welcoming visitors to the market town of Street carries an illustration of an ichthyosaur because fossils of this reptile were found in a local quarry in 1884. Quarrying in Street was a major industry until the start of the twentieth century, when it declined as bricks were a cheaper option. As numerous ichthyosaur fossils were found in the quarries, Street Urban District Council adopted the marine reptile as its emblem. It's still the symbol of Street. Many of the fossils excavated in Street are today displayed at the Natural History Museum in London.

THE SOMERSET HIGHWAY

There are 4,206 miles of road throughout Somerset, including the M5 motorway. The stretch of road with the highest traffic volume, perhaps unsurprisingly, is the M5 between Junctions 24 and 25, with more than 166 million vehicle miles per year.

The M5 Avonmouth Bridge carries traffic over the River Avon from Bristol into Somerset and vice versa. The eight-lane bridge cost £4.2 million, and when it was opened in May 1974 it meant the end of the Pill Ferry. For many centuries a ferry carried commuters from the north Somerset village of Pill across the River Avon to the Bristol suburb of Shirehampton, where a bus would take them into the centre of the city.

Porlock Hill, Exmoor, with a gradient approaching 1 in 4 (25 per cent), is part of the A39 and the steepest A-road in the United Kingdom. It connects Porlock to Lynmouth and Barnstaple in Devon. The hill is made up of chicanes, hairpin bends and straight sections of road.

The first maps of Somerset produced by the Ordnance Survey were published in 1802 with a scale of 1in to 1 mile.

SOMERSET IN FLOWER

The county flower of Somerset is the Cheddar Pink, which was discovered 300 years ago. It grows in several places in the Mendip Hills but nowhere more profusely than on the limestone rocks in the Cheddar Gorge. This scented pink grows up to a foot tall and normally flowers in June and July.

The first published mention of Cheddar Pinks is from 1696, when a Mr Brewer reported that the flower had been found 'On Chidderoks in Somersetshire'. It is so rare – the Cheddar Pink is endemic to Cheddar – that it is a legally protected plant.

Vivary Park, a green oasis in Taunton town centre, gets its name from its use as a complex of fishponds known as a vivarium when the land was owned by the Bishop of Winchester in the twelfth century. It is the home of Taunton Flower Show – now known as the Chelsea of the West – which was first held here in 1851.

LAST OF ITS KIND

Stembridge Tower Mill is England's last remaining thatched windmill. The four-storey tower, which was built in 1822, can be found in the village of High Ham near Langport. The mill was given a restoration by local craftsmen in 2000 costing £100,000. Although the sails do not turn with the wind, they are moved 90 degrees four times a year for maintenance. The tower is owned by the National Trust and is a Grade II* listed building. It was last used in 1910.

CELEBRATING THE COUNTY

Somerset Day is celebrated on 11 May with various events taking place all over the county. The organisation behind the special day, Passion for Somerset, is a not-for-profit Community Interest Company. It champions the single aim of celebrating Somerset and all that the county has to offer. The organisers say the celebrations are in honour of King Alfred the Great's routing of the Vikings from his stronghold in the Somerset marshes in May 878.

Two of Somerset's bridges – Pulteney Bridge over the River Avon at Bath, built in 1774, and the medieval 120ft-long Tarr Steps bridge, which crosses the River Barle in Exmoor – were featured on postage stamps issued by the Royal Mail in 1968. They were part of a set of ten stamps celebrating Britain's engineering feats.

A booklet issued by the Great Western Railway in 1931 tempting holidaymakers to spend time in Somerset was titled 'Smiling Somerset'. The county now attracts an annual 11.4 million day visitors and 1.8 million overnight visitors from within Great Britain.

Council records show that today more than 20,000 people throughout the county depend on tourism as their sole source of income.

AND FINALLY ...

The marriage record of Anne Holbrook and James Hilliar at Walcot St Swithin in Bath in March 1794 says that 'the man came so drunk as not to be able to repeat the words of the ceremony'. It meant the actual marriage had to take place the following month.

Another wedding record details the marriage of a very interesting pair in Yatton in 1762, that of Sage and Onion – Samuel Sage and Hannah Onion.

A blue plaque in the centre of Chard marks an unusual event. It marks the occasion that the husband of Lizzie Taff sold her for half a crown in 1801. Wife selling in England was a way of ending an unsatisfactory marriage by mutual agreement that probably began in the late seventeenth century, when divorce was a practical impossibility for all but the very wealthiest.

2

BESIDE THE SEASIDE

PORTISHEAD

Portishead, a small coastal town in north Somerset, had a long history of being a fishing village. However, early in the nineteenth century it began to develop as a seaside resort. At the same time, industry began to prosper. The Victorian period saw day trippers arriving at Portishead by paddle steamer. An approach golf course opened in 1908 and two years later the Lake Grounds, once a stagnant stretch of rhynes [drainage ditches], was dug out by unemployed men. It is still used for activities like boating, canoeing and even paddling.

Ladies Only Beach
In the middle of the nineteenth century Portishead had a bathing beach for women only, complete with a robing salon and a female attendant. A beach for men was further along the sea front.

Resort's New Attraction
The Royal Pier Hotel was built in 1831 by Bristol Corporation, which was keen to make Portishead a retreat for wealthy businessmen who wanted to get away from the grime, smoke and noise of the industrial city. It is thought to be the only seaside hotel developed by a public authority in the nineteenth century. The Royal Pier Hotel was sold in the latter part of the twentieth

century and today carries on as the Royal Inn, a privately run venture.

Off-shore Training School
The training ship *Formidable* was anchored 400 yards off the Portishead seafront for more than forty years. It was used to train boys in need of care and protection to lead useful lives. Many of them were homeless and had been found wandering the streets of Bristol. When the ship became unseaworthy in 1906, businessman Henry Fedden built a training school on land in nearby Nore Road. The Grade II listed building is now a gated development of apartments, houses and maisonettes, appropriately called Fedden Village.

Dockland Regeneration
Portishead still gets lots of visitors but the town has been transformed. Its deep-water docks, built in the 1860s to receive cargoes from all over the world, were closed in 1992. The area has since been developed into a marina where 400 leisure craft are moored alongside a residential area. Apartments and houses now occupy the dockside sites of a phosphorous works and two power stations, which have all been demolished as part of a multi-million pound regeneration scheme.

Large ocean-going vessels pass closer to the land at Battery Point, Portishead, than to any other part of the United Kingdom's coastline.

CLEVEDON

Poetic Praise for Clevedon
Clevedon, which stands on the Bristol Channel coastline, has the genteel air of a Victorian residential town. It lacks the

razzmataz of other seaside towns but is probably best known for its Victorian pier, about which Sir John Betjeman, Poet Laureate, broadcaster and writer on architecture, waxed lyrical: 'It recalls a painting by Turner, or an etching by Whistler or Sickert, or even a Japanese print. Without its pier, Clevedon would be a diamond with a flaw.'

A Pier For the Town

Clevedon Pier was built in less than two years from surplus rail track belonging to the South Wales Railway. The wrought iron was fashioned into the elegant spans that are still a feature of the pier. Clevedon Pier was designed to receive passengers arriving on the paddle steamers from Devon and Wales – thus boosting the town's economy. The pier cost £10,000 and it was built at the height of Victorian engineering. It was the twenty-fifth of sixty-three piers constructed in England between 1813 and 1891.

Gala Opening for Pier

Clevedon Pier was opened on Easter Monday 1869 amidst a fanfare of music from five bands and a procession from the railway station to the pier that included uniformed policemen and 500 schoolchildren, who sang the 148th Psalm. A cannon volley was fired by the First Somerset Artillery and ballad-mongers burst into song. The next day the town's weekly paper, the *Clevedon Mercury,* published a special edition in which it said the opening of the pier gave the town 'the greatest day Clevedon has ever experienced'. The spectacular occasion also attracted national coverage in the *Illustrated London News*. The people of Clevedon grew to love their pier so much that in 1913 local clergyman the Rev. Charles Marson of St Andrew's church was prompted to say: 'Clevedon without a pier would be like a dog without a tail.' In the *Visitors' Handbook to Clevedon* published around 1890, the editor wrote: 'Clevedon Pier is a favourite promenade with visitors, as there they can derive all the salutary advantages of the pure sea air without any risk of the dreaded nausea.'

Disaster Hits the Pier

For more than a century the pier withstood the raging 42ft high tides of the Bristol Channel. But disaster struck while safety tests for insurance purposes were being carried out in October 1970. The two end spans of the pier collapsed into the Bristol Channel. It meant that the pier-head, with its pagoda-like pavilion, remained isolated in the Bristol Channel. It stayed like that for more than a decade while the pier's owners, Woodspring District Council, argued that it was dangerous and should be destroyed. The council's view brought protests from pier-lovers all over the country, who claimed that the dramatic landmark should be restored and kept as a national monument. Architects added to the argument, saying that the pier's eight spans of iron and the tracery-work make it one of the most graceful in the country. Thousands of people attended fund-raising events and signed petitions and the poet John Betjeman lent his support.

The Government Intervenes

The future of the pier literally hung in the balance until the government held a public inquiry in 1980. It lasted three days and after hearing all the evidence the inquiry inspector advised the Minister for the Environment that the 1,024ft-long pier should be restored. Grants from various local and national organisations enabled repairs and restoration to get under way. Clevedon Pier was formally reopened by Sir Charles Elton, great-great-grandson of the original chairman of the Clevedon Pier Company, and the well-known Clevedon bowler David Bryant. Ten years later the pier was awarded the honour of Pier of the Year by the National Piers Society. In 2001 the pier was upgraded from a Grade II* listed structure to Grade I.

Literary Honeymoon Hotspot
After marrying Sarah Fricker at Bristol in 1795, the Romantic poet Samuel Taylor Coleridge took his bride to Clevedon for their honeymoon. They spent two months living in a cottage in Old Church Road. While there Coleridge completed his poem 'The Eolian Harp'. In 1916 the author J.R.R. Tolkien, well-known for his books *The Lord of the Rings* and *The Hobbit*, also honeymooned at Clevedon. Tolkien and his bride, Emma, spent a week there, which included a visit to Cheddar Caves.

WESTON-SUPER-MARE

The Resort With 'Air Like Wine'
The fishing village of Weston-super-Mare started to gain popularity in the mid-eighteenth century when doctors were extolling the virtues of drinking and bathing in sea water. When doctors recommended that their patients take what became known as the 'sea-cure', Weston-super-Mare was the nearest coastal village within easy reach of people living in Bath and Bristol. It became so popular that a visitors' guidebook was published in 1822. For the accommodation of visitors there was one hotel, a couple of inns and some lodging houses. Available for their entertainment was a billiard table, reading room and two pleasure boats that could be hired. By the early 1920s posters that advertised the delights of the resort declared that Weston-super-Mare had 'air like wine'.

Weston's First Pier

There was more for visitors to do when Birnbeck Pier was built. This is the only pier in the country that connects the mainland to an island – Birnbeck. This is a rocky island of just 3 acres. Birnbeck Pier, a Grade II* listed pier, dates back to 1867. It is now derelict and has been closed to visitors since 1994 awaiting possible rebuilding. The pier is now on the Buildings at Risk Register. In its heyday the 1,000ft-long Birnbeck Pier received thousands of visitors to Weston, who arrived by paddle steamer from South Wales. At one time this amounted to 750,000 people a year. They could use the pier's slot machines, which dispensed such things as scents, matches and even a cup of tea. However, in the 1930s Birnbeck's popularity started to decline, especially after a funfair had opened on the rival Grand Pier.

Seafront Improvements

Work started in 1833 on a stone-built promenade for Weston-super-Mare's seafront, at a cost of £30,000. It was described at the time as the biggest civil engineering project of its kind in the South-West, taking three years to complete. Today, many thousands of visitors from the United Kingdom and far beyond stroll along the promenade of what is now Somerset's largest seaside resort.

A Rival Pier

The Grand Pier was built less than a mile along the coast from Birnbeck Pier in 1904, at a cost of £120,000, and stands at the centre of the town's 2-mile long promenade. The 2,000-seat theatre at the end of the pier was popular not only with visitors but also the town's residents. They could enjoy Shakespearean productions, opera, ballet, music hall events and boxing matches. At night the pier was illuminated by 1,500 electric lamps. When the Grand Pier was built there was a plan to run regular paddle steamer services to Cardiff but the tide and strong currents made the mooring of ships too dangerous, so the idea was dropped.

Fire Wrecks the Pier
Disaster struck the pier in 1930 when the pavilion was destroyed by fire. It turned out that the pier was under-insured and its owners had to find £36,000 to pay for it to be rebuilt. The pier was completely reopened in 1933 and instead of a theatre the pavilion housed an undercover funfair.

History Repeats Itself
Fire struck again in 2008, completely destroying the pavilion. Eighty-five firefighters fought the blaze, which took hold of the partly wooden pier early on the morning of 28 July.

Black smoke could be seen more than 10 miles away. Fire investigators said the blaze had started in an area containing deep fat fryers. The 1,201ft-long pier was revamped at a staggering cost of £39 million and reopened two years later. It is now supported by 360 original cast iron piles from 1904 and seventy-one new steel piles that were added during the rebuild in 2010. The pier was formally reopened by the Princess Royal, Princess Anne.

New Owners for the Pier

The Grand Pier was owned by the Brenner family from 1946 until 2008. when it was bought in a multi-million pound deal by brother and sister partnership Michelle and Kerry Michael. The pier, which is a Grade II listed building, has twice been awarded the title of Pier of the Year, firstly in 2002 and again in 2011, by the National Piers Society.

Donkey Rides

Donkeys have been a major seaside attraction at Weston-super-Mare since 1886, when beach rides were set up by the Mager family. The same family has been working on the sands giving donkey rides to children ever since. Most of the Magers' fifty donkeys are home bred and have the luxury of only working from Easter to October. The rest of the year they spend their holidays on various farms in the area, where they are thoroughly spoilt by local children. The donkeys, wearing a sun hat, have had pride of place on the cover of Weston-super-Mare's annual holiday guide.

'Dismaland' Comes to Town

The resort's holiday trade got a big boost in 2015 when Britain's best-known and most prolific street artist, Banksy, took over the disused seafront lido for five weeks. He created ten new works of his own and invited other artists to join him in the exhibition,

which was called Dismaland. The pop-up exhibition, which had been prepared in secrecy, ran for thirty-six days. Banksy described it as a 'family theme park unsuitable for children'. Nearly 200,000 people, many from overseas, visited the show, which gave the Weston-super-Mare economy an estimated boost of £20 million. It was Banksy's first show in the United Kingdom since he took over Bristol Museum for a three-month exhibition in 2009.

Beach Lawns Battle

The Beach Lawns on the seafront were the venue for such events as vintage car shows and the annual Dairy Festival, which drew thousands of visitors to the resort. But in the 1970s the Beach Lawns were the scene of Bank Holiday clashes between sharp-suited Mods and Rockers in their black leather and denim.

Holiday Guide Ban

Weston-super-Mare claimed to be the first resort in the country to ban the word 'guinea' from hotel advertisements. From 1966, the resort's official guidebook would only list prices in pounds, shillings and pence. The town council's publicity officer said 'this fictitious unit of currency was confusing to the foreign visitors we are endeavouring to attract'. The name guinea was used to indicate the amount of 21*s* and was first used in 1663. In decimal currency this is £1.05. A guinea was close to a pound, so putting prices in guineas made the price seem less.

AN ISLAND STEEPED IN HISTORY

From Barracks to Nature Reserve

Six miles out into the Bristol Channel off Weston-super-Mare is the tiny island of Steep Holm. It had its own role in two world wars but today is a barren and rocky island nature reserve and bird sanctuary. It rises to about 200ft from sea level and covers 49 acres at high tide. However, at low tide it expands to 63 acres. This is due to the tidal range of 43ft, the second highest in the world after the Bay of Fundy in eastern Canada. In 1976 the Kenneth Allsop Memorial Trust bought Steep Holm for £10,000 in memory of the broadcaster and naturalist of that name. The Trust said its aim was: 'To protect, preserve and enhance for the benefit of the public the landscape, antiquities, flora, fauna, natural beauty and scientific interest of the island of Steep Holm in the County of Somerset.' Victorian barracks on the island have been turned into a visitor centre. Steep Holm is part of Somerset and comes under the administration of North Somerset Council.

BURNHAM-ON-SEA

About 8 miles south of Weston-super-Mare is Burnham-on-Sea, which was originally seen as a rival resort. Its esplanade is lined with Victorian and Edwardian guest houses looking out on what is said to be the shortest pier in the country at just 117ft long. It was built in 1911–14 and was the first British marine building to be constructed in ferro-concrete, a French invention. The pier was designed to serve as a jetty for a steamer service linking the railway with Wales. However, there were problems with silt and the idea was short-lived. The pier stands in the centre of Burnham's esplanade and its pavilion is occupied by an amusement arcade. At the end of 2017 the family that had owned the pier for forty-nine years announced that it had been sold to new owners for an undisclosed amount. In 2008 the pier was rated amongst the top five in Britain by the *Daily Express*.

Golden Sands

The stretch of sand between Burnham-on-Sea in the south and Brean Down in the north is 7 miles long. It is one of the longest expanses of sand in Europe.

Local Vicar Turns the Town into a Spa Resort

In the early nineteenth century an entrepreneurial Church of England vicar built a spa complex near his church. The Reverend David Davies, who was the curate for Burnham, Berrow and Brean, had two health-giving mineral water wells sunk at what is now known as Steart House on The Esplanade. One well was 75ft deep and the other 25ft. The waters were chalybeate and sulphurous. Bath and pump rooms were provided in the house for patients. After the Rev. Davies died, the spa's new owner tried to develop a larger scheme but it failed. Steart House is now a Grade II listed building and has been converted into flats.

Jetty Disaster

A jetty built on the seafront at Burnham-on-Sea in 1857 by a local entrepreneur and businessman George Reed was intended to serve passenger and commercial traffic to and from South Wales. Unfortunately, the first ship from Barry, the *Iron Duke*, came to grief in mud. Today, the jetty plays an important role in launching the town's sea rescue services.

Lighthouses Galore

Burnham-on-Sea's High Lighthouse – it is 110ft high – was the first lighthouse to become fully automated. It was designed and built by Joseph Nelson in the 1830s. It was equipped with a paraffin lamp, which shone through a half-gallery under a window. The lighthouse was deactivated in the early 1990s and sold by the Trinity House Corporation, which is the governing authority for lighthouses in England, to a private buyer. The eight-storey building has since been converted into residential accommodation with one circular room on each of its eight floors.

The existing lighthouse is a white-painted wooden square building that sits on nine stilts or pillars, some of them with metal plates for reinforcement. The building stands on the beach and, besides being a navigational aid, is also a popular tourist attraction that is visited by many thousands of walkers each year. The lighthouse-on-legs, as visitors refer to it, provides shipping with a flashing light every 7.5 seconds.

However, Burnham's lighthouse story goes way back to 1750 when a fisherman's wife was worried that her husband had not come home by dark. She put a lit candle in the window of their cottage and her husband eventually returned home safely. Sailors paid the woman small sums of money to keep the candle burning, so they too could find their way home. At one time a light burning on the top of the tower of St Andrew's Church also acted as a lighthouse.

MINEHEAD

This is west Somerset's main resort. Minehead once had a pier but it was demolished after about forty years. The 700ft-long pier opened in 1901, at a cost of £12,000. It had four landing stages for paddle steamers, which took day-trippers on Bristol Channel cruises to resorts in other parts of Somerset, north Devon, Lundy Island in the Bristol Channel and South Wales. The pier was demolished in 1940 to allow nearby gun batteries a clear line of sight across the channel in the Second World War. This was the only seaside pier in the country to be knocked down to aid the war effort. Compensation of £90,000 was awarded to the owners, P. and A. Campbell, the firm that was also the main paddle-steamer operator in the Bristol Channel. The firm used the compensation to improve its steamer fleet.

Beach Washed Away
The north-facing sand and shingle beach at Minehead was almost completely washed away in 1990 by a heavy storm. The Environment Agency designed a £12.6 million sea defence scheme to reduce the risk of this erosion and flooding happening again. This included building a new sea wall of just over a mile

long and importing 320,000 tons of additional sand in 1999 to build a new beach.

A 'Rare Find' at Minehead

One of the most unusual sights at Minehead is the wreckage of a wooden sailing vessel, but it can only be seen when winter storms remove the sand under which it is buried. English Heritage has declared the wreckage of the *Bristol Packet* as being of 'national importance' and said that its discovery was a 'rare find'. It has also granted the remains of the American-built fully rigged vessel lying at Madbrain Sands 'protected status'. The ship, which was made of pine and larch, was lost on a coastal voyage from Teignmouth to Bristol in 1808.

Coastline Walk

The South West Coast Path starts in Minehead, follows the Exmoor coast and finishes at Poole Harbour in Dorset. It is the longest National Trail in England and Wales at 630 miles. The path was originally created by coastguards who were patrolling the south-west peninsula checking every inlet for smugglers. Their route is the basis for the coast walk. Walking the entire route will take seven to eight weeks.

3

HISTORY, MYSTERY, MYTH AND LEGEND

A CENTRE OF PILGRIMAGE

From time immemorial the market town of Glastonbury has been a magnet for Christian pilgrims, mystics and historians from all over the world. It is a place where it is difficult to separate history and mystery. This small town abounds in ancient legends, traditions, a concentration of medieval buildings, monuments and numerous shops concentrating on New Age cults. It has all played its part in turning Glastonbury into an international tourist attraction.

Cradle of Christianity

Glastonbury has long been described as the 'cradle of Christianity' in this country. Legend has it that Joseph of Arimathea, said to be the Virgin Mary's uncle, was a trader who travelled to Somerset with the young Jesus. On a return visit after Jesus had been crucified, Joseph of Arimathea is said to have built the first Christian church in England. It was made of wattle and daub and it is said that the site Joseph chose for his place of worship later became the Lady Chapel of Glastonbury Abbey.

A Royal Tradition

Legend also has it that Joseph planted his walking staff on Wearyall Hill where it miraculously took root and flowered into a tree that has since become known as the Holy Thorn. It flowers twice a year to recall the birth and death of Christ and the bringing of Christianity to our islands. It has become a custom that a sprig, or cutting, is sent to the queen as a decoration for her Christmas table each year. This is a tradition that is believed to date back to the days when James Montague, Bishop of Bath and Wells, sent a cutting from the Holy Thorn to Queen Anne, the consort of James I (1566–1625). Every December local schoolchildren watch as Glastonbury's Mayor and the Vicar of Glastonbury ceremonially cut sprigs from the tree to send to the queen.

Holy Thorn Damaged

In December 2010 vandals used a chainsaw to cut the Holy Thorn on Wearyall Hill down to a stump of about 18in, prompting a police investigation. Two years later the replacement tree was again cut down by vandals. However, Glastonbury is not without its important tree. Descendants of the original Holy Thorn were planted long ago in the grounds of Glastonbury Abbey, the gardens of the Chalice Well and the grounds of the town's Rural Life Museum.

The Holy Grail

Legend has it that Joseph of Arimathea also buried the Holy Grail, or the Chalice that Jesus used at the Last Supper, in the area now known as the Chalice Well at the foot of Glastonbury Tor. It is one of Britain's most ancient wells and is also known as the Red Spring. Water issues from the spring at a rate of 250,000 imperial gallons per day. It has never dried up, even during drought. Iron oxide deposits give the water a reddish hue. Like the hot springs in Bath, the water from the Chalice Well is reputed to possess healing qualities.

GLASTONBURY ABBEY

Glastonbury Abbey was founded in the seventh century and enlarged three centuries later. When the Domesday Book was commissioned to provide records and a census of life in England, the abbey was revealed to be one of the wealthiest and most important monasteries in England. It had its own farms, library and workshops.

Disaster struck the abbey in 1184 when fire badly damaged the building. Many of the abbey's ancient treasures were destroyed. Beaten but not bowed, the monks set about rebuilding their abbey.

The Abbey's Fish House

The only surviving monastic fishery building in England can be found at Meare, a village not far from Glastonbury. The Fish House was built around the 1330s by Glastonbury Abbey as a home for the official in charge of the nearby fishery – a freshwater lake providing food for the staff of the abbey. The Fish House can still be visited.

Abbey's Royal Funerals

Such was the importance of Glastonbury Abbey that three kings – Edmund, Edgar and Edmund Ironside – were buried there.

Dissolution of the Monasteries

In 1536 there were more than 800 monasteries, nunneries and friaries in Britain. Five years later there were none. The Dissolution of the Monasteries carried out by Henry VIII meant that more than 10,000 monks and nuns had been dispersed and the buildings they used had been seized by the Crown to be sold off or leased to new lay occupiers. Glastonbury Abbey was one of the principal victims of this action by the king.

Abbey's Pilgrimages

At one time the abbey ruins, which stand in 36 acres of parkland, were privately owned but since 1908 they have been in the ownership of the Church of England, which stages an annual one-day pilgrimage. It is held on the Saturday after the Feast Day of St John the Baptist, while a Roman Catholic pilgrimage usually takes place later. In the style of traditional pilgrimages, some of the people taking part walk 23 miles from Bristol to Glastonbury. Many go on to climb Glastonbury Tor. A service that is held in the abbey grounds is relayed by loudspeakers to the crowds.

ST DUNSTAN

One of the abbey's best-known abbots came from Somerset. St Dunstan, who was born at nearby Baltonsborough, became a scholar, craftsman and statesman. He was educated at the abbey and appointed its abbot in 945. His work restored monastic life in England and reformed the English Church. While he was Abbot of Glastonbury, St Dunstan was responsible for enlarging the church. He was later successively created Bishop of Worcester and Bishop of London, and in 959 King Edgar appointed him as Archbishop of Canterbury. He was later canonised as a saint.

ABBEY'S LAST ABBOT

The last abbot of Glastonbury Abbey was Richard Whiting (1461–1539), another Somerset man. He presided over the abbey at the time of the Dissolution of the Monasteries. Whiting was hanged for treason, along with two of his monks, on the summit of Glastonbury Tor on the king's orders after he had been convicted of remaining loyal to Rome.

KING ARTHUR: FACT OR FICTION?

It is in Glastonbury that King Arthur and Queen Guinevere are reputed to have been laid to rest. At the time this was still an island known as the Isle of Avalon. Legend has it that King Arthur was brought here in a boat after being wounded in his last battle.

In 1191 the remains of the couple were said to have been found in the cemetery at the abbey, south of the Lady Chapel.

One story has it that in order to raise extra funds from pilgrims to pay for the rebuilding the abbey after the fire the monks dug to find the remains of the king and his queen. It was claimed that they found a stone bearing the inscription 'Here lies Arthur, King'. The monks raised the bones of two bodies – one male and the other female – from a deep grave. These bones were reburied, much later, in 1278 within the abbey church, in a black marble tomb. Apparently, this was done amidst much ceremony in the presence of King Edward I. When the abbey was sacked and largely destroyed in the Dissolution the caskets were lost and they have never been found. Today all that marks the spot of what is said to be King Arthur's final resting place is a noticeboard.

GLASTONBURY LANDMARK

Glastonbury Tor, standing sentinel-like over the town and nearby area, is shrouded in its own myths and legends. On a clear day the 518ft-high conical Tor can be seen from as far as 20 miles away. On its summit are the ruins of a fifteenth-century church tower. These are the only remains of St Michael's church that once stood on the site. A plaque on the tower tells those with sturdy legs who have managed to climb the Tor 'that in legend the earliest reference (to the Tor) is a mid-thirteenth century story of St Patrick's return from Ireland in which he became leader of a group of hermits at Glastonbury and discovered an ancient ruined oratory on the summit after climbing through a dense wood'. Glastonbury Tor is owned and managed by the National Trust.

CHURCH CONTROVERSY

The war memorial in front of St John's parish church in the High Street was designed by Bligh Bond, an architect, illustrator, archaeologist and psychical researcher. He used the design of a Saxon cross that he discovered when excavating in Glastonbury Abbey. His work in the ruins started soon after the abbey was bought by the Church of England in 1908. Bond was sacked by the church authorities after revealing that his research was based on the spirit writing of a medieval monk.

'NEW AGE' GLASTONBURY

Besides the church-organised pilgrimages each summer, many individuals and groups of various beliefs and faiths are now attracted to the town. The Pilgrim Reception Centre says that more than seventy different faiths are practised in Glastonbury. According to the centre, this is a greater concentration per capita than anywhere else in the world.

SOME GLASTONBURY FAITHS

Classical Devotional Polytheism
This is dedicated to the Theoi (Greco–Roman Deities) and Numina. For those with a 'deeply devotional relationship to the manifold Divine and with the reverence for animal life embodied in Pythagorean philosophy' there is a discussion group and a Votive Temple and prayer garden in the town.

Glastonbury Goddess Temple and the Goddess Hall

The temple mainly celebrates goddesses who are particularly associated with Glastonbury and the Isle of Avalon. Glastonbury also hosts an annual goddess conference attended by people from all over the world.

Glastonbury Pagan Moot

A 'Glastonbury Under the Stars' pagan gathering, the Moot is held once a month, when people interested in the Pagan tradition get together. Open rituals are also held in Glastonbury to celebrate the equinoxes.

Gorsedh Ynis Witrin

The primary focus of this faith is to support, promote and honour Pan-Celtic culture, spirituality and creativity within the local community. An annual competition is held to decide the next Bard of Glastonbury. There is also a yearly Open Gorsedh ceremony at which the new Bards are publicly invested.

OBOD (Order of Bards, Ovates & Druids)

Obod holds a yearly pre-summer Solstice ceremony on the summit of Glastonbury Tor.

The White Spring

The White Spring is open regularly for all to visit and holds new moon and full moon meditations, rituals and healing circles, and celebrates the sabbats (the festivals of the wheel of the year).

RETAIL THERAPY

Very few national traders are represented in Glastonbury's town centre. Instead, dozens of local and independent New

Age mystics and spiritual healers rub shoulders with each other selling everything from polished pebbles to crystals and from complementary medicine to spiritual books.

Seven Town-Centre Traders and Some of Their Products:
   The Goddess and the Green Man (book-seller)
   Star Child Glastonbury (Herb shop)
   Enlightened Gift Shop
   Earthfare Glastonbury (Health foods retailer)
   The Cat and Cauldron (Gift shop with hand-crafted artefacts from the Pagan community).
   Maid in Glastonbury (Sells items from antlered headdresses to Green Man/Woman masks and books).
   The Crystal Man (Items include minerals, silver and crystals).

SOME OTHER MYTHS AND LEGENDS

King Arthur's Camelot
Legend has long maintained that the Iron Age hill fort at South Cadbury in south Somerset was the site of King Arthur's Camelot and where his castle stood.

Baking the Cakes
Probably the best known legend or myth about Alfred the Great – the only English monarch to have the title 'Great' – concerns the time he was seeking refuge from the invading Danes on the Somerset Levels. He had taken lodgings with a peasant woman who is said to have asked him to look after the cakes she was baking near the fire in her hut at Athelney. The story goes that King Alfred's mind wandered on to more pressing matters, letting the cakes burn. He was scolded by the woman.

The Bishop's Dream

The first sight most visitors have of Bath Abbey is of its west front, with its unique ladders of angels. It is said that the plans behind this design were first thought up by the Bishop of Bath and Wells, Oliver King. The story goes that one night he had a dream about angels ascending and descending above him. Building work on the church started around 1499 but wasn't completed for another 120 years.

The Saint on a Raft

St Decuman's church, Watchet, is dedicated to a Celtic saint who is said to have travelled from South Wales across the Bristol Channel on a raft with a cow for a companion. He came ashore at Watchet on the west Somerset coast in the seventh century. St Decuman is said to have healed the sick and acted as a pastor to the people of Watchet.

Jack Horner and the King's Pie

The Horner family in Mells are claimed by some to be the descendants of Jack in the nursery rhyme 'Little Jack Horner'. According to legend, Jack Horner was the steward to the last Abbot of Glastonbury Abbey, and helped himself to the deeds of the manors of Mells, Nunney and Leigh on Mendip. Legend has it that they had been hidden in a pie that was to be sent to King Henry VIII after the Dissolution of the Monasteries.

The Peril of Going to the Well ...

Jack and Jill Lane in the small village of Kilmersdon between Radstock and Frome is said to have been where Jack, of Jack and Jill of nursery rhyme fame, met his fate. In 2000 the villagers had a lead plaque fixed to the wall of Kilmersdon Primary School commemorating the couple. Part of the inscription says that while collecting water from a well, Jack was hit by a boulder from a nearby quarry. He tumbled down and suffered a wound that even vinegar and brown paper could not mend. Jill also died young but not before giving birth to the couple's son, who was brought up by villagers and called Jill's son. According to the plaque, which overlooks a well, the surname Gilson still features in the area.

The Witch of Wookey

According to legend, the village of Wookey Hole, close to Wells, was once home to a famous witch, who cursed a man from Glastonbury who was betrothed to a girl from Wookey. The man unsuccessfully sought revenge. Some people believe that the witch continues to haunt relationships in the village today.

4

THEY PUT SOMERSET ON THE MAP

Abelard, who was born in Bath around 1080, was a mathematician renowned for his role in the introduction of Hindu/Arabic numerals and the concept of zero to the Western world.

Actress Jenny Agutter was born in Taunton in 1952. She began her career as a child actress in 1964, appearing *in East of Sudan*, and two adaptations of *The Railway Children* – the BBC's 1968 television serial and the 1970 film version. She also starred in the TV film *The Snow Goose*, for which she won an Emmy Award for Outstanding Supporting Actress in a Drama. Jenny Agutter continues to work in television drama and has appeared in the series *Call the Midwife*.

Paddy (now Lord) Ashdown of Yeovil married local girl Jane Courtney at St Andrew's church, Burnham-on-Sea, in 1961. He was Yeovil's Member of Parliament from 1983 to 2001.Ashdown was leader of the Liberal Democrat party for eleven years until 1999. Before fighting his first General Election, Paddy Ashdown was a Royal Marine and Special Boat Service officer. He also served as an intelligence officer in the UK security services.

From farmer's boy to Minister of the Crown sounds like something out of a paperback novel but this was the true life story of Ernest Bevin. He left school when he was 11 and worked as a farm labourer in his home village of Winsford, Exmoor.

After a variety of other jobs he began to take an interest in politics and became an organiser for the dockers' union. Bevin (1881–1951) later became General Secretary of the Transport and General Workers Union. In 1940 he was appointed Minister of Labour and National Service in Winston Churchill's coalition government and Foreign Secretary in the Labour government of 1945–51.

Walter Bagehot (1826–77), who was born in Langport, became an influential economist and journalist. He edited the highly respected magazine *The Economist* and wrote a number of books on economics and politics. His *English Constitution*, published in 1867, was regarded as a standard work. His life is commemorated in Langport by a stained glass window in All Saints church, which was donated by his widow, Eliza. Walter Bagehot is buried in the churchyard.

Horace Batchelor (1899–1977) certainly put his home town of Keynsham on the map when he advertised his own system of predicting football match results. He gave it the grand name of the Infra Draw method. Batchelor also created his own adverts for Radio Luxembourg in the 1950s and 1960s – the only commercial radio station on the air at the time. He made sure that money from listeners who wanted to take part in his scheme was sent to the right address by spelling it out. The address was always read on air as 'Horace Batchelor, Department One, Keynsham, spelt K-E-Y-N-S-H-A-M, Keynsham, Bristol'. Contemporary newspaper reports said that he helped gamblers win more than £12 million between 1948 and 1971. No one knows, though, how much Batchelor made himself, although he was described by newspapers as a 'millionaire'.

The Bath-born television baker Mary Berry was awarded the freedom of her native city in June 2014. After leaving Bath High School, she enrolled at Bath College of Domestic Science and later trained at The Cordon Bleu in Paris. Apart from her television work, Berry has written more than sixty books about cookery.

Margaret Bondfield (1873–1953) who was born at Hunt's Place in Chard was a suffragette, a member of Parliament, the first woman to become a member of the Cabinet as Minister of Labour in 1929 and the first female in the United Kingdom to become a Privy Counsellor. After leaving school when she was 13 years old, Bondfield worked in a shop and became interested in trade union activities. She was eventually appointed chair of the General Council of the Trades Union Congress. A blue plaque on the wall of the Guildhall at Chard commemorates her life and career.

Motor racing driver Jenson Button (1980–) was born and brought up in Frome. He took up karting when he was just 8 years old. Button won his first Grand Prix in Hungary in 2006 and three years later won the FIA Formula One championship. He became a director of the Grand Prix Drivers' Association, the union with a focus upon safety in motorsport, in 2013. Button has been given the freedom of Frome, and a street in the town is named after him. Ironically, he failed his driving test the first time and had to retake it.

The Rt Reverend George Carey was Bishop of Bath and Wells 1987–91. His next appointment was that of Archbishop of Canterbury, a post he held for ten years. During his time as archbishop, the Church of England ordained its first women priests, although the actual ordination service of the first thirty-two women priests took place at Bristol Cathedral and not Canterbury.

From the age of 16 until she was 19 years old, Edith Cavell (1865–1915) attended three boarding schools in different parts of the country, one of them being in Clevedon. She also went to St Andrew's church, where she was confirmed in 1884.

Cavell later trained as a nurse but was shot by the Germans for helping Allied fugitives to escape.

Stella Clarke (1932–) has been active in public life for more than sixty years. She was one of the youngest councillors in the country when she joined the long defunct Long Ashton Rural District Council when she was 23 years old. An interest in children's welfare and housing led Clarke, who lives in Long Ashton, to spend twenty years on Somerset County Council as a co-opted member. In the early 1970s she and her late husband, Charles, bought and restored the Theatre Royal at Bath. Clarke has worked with many national and local bodies and one of her latest projects involves helping former soldiers to build their own homes.

John Cleese, who co-founded Monty Python, the comedy troupe responsible for the TV sketch show *Monty Python's Flying Circus* and four Monty Python films, was born in Weston-super-Mare. He attended St Peter's Preparatory School in the town. Amongst his many activities in the world of show business, Cleese co-wrote and starred in the sitcom *Fawlty Towers*, for which he received the 1980 BAFTA for Best Entertainment Performance. His father's name was originally Reginald Cheese.

Although he served for a time in the navy, William Dampier, who was born at Hymerford House near Yeovil in 1651, spent much of his career as a pirate. In one expedition, Dampier, who was educated at King's School, Bruton, seized a ship at Sierra Leone and sailed the Pacific Ocean, reaching the Philippines, Australia and China. He was also an explorer and made three voyages around the world. Dampier also wrote books about his travels in which he gave precise details of oceanography.

Jill Dando (1961–99) started her journalistic career as a trainee reporter on her home town local weekly paper, the *Weston Mercury*. The *Mercury* played a large part in the life of the Dando family as Jill's father was senior compositor on the paper and her brother Nigel was a reporter before moving onto an evening paper and later into local radio. After five years as a newspaper journalist Jill moved to the BBC, initially as a regional presenter and then nationally. In 1997 she was BBC Personality of the Year and is best remembered for her work on the *Crimewatch* and *Holiday* programmes. Tragically, Dando was murdered on the doorstep of her home in London in 1999. So far nobody has been convicted of the killing.

The explorer Sir Ranulph Twisleton-Wykeham Fiennes (1944–), who lives on a farm on Exmoor, is not someone to turn down a challenge. Between 1969 and 1986 he led six major expeditions, including a journey up the White Nile by hovercraft. Sir Ranulph was the first man to reach both poles and to cross the Arctic and Antarctic oceans. He once removed his frostbitten fingertips with a fretsaw. Sir Ranulph ran seven marathons in seven days, and that was just four months after suffering a heart attack. One of the books he has written is aptly titled *Living Dangerously.*

Keith Floyd (1943–2009), restaurant owner, television chef and author, was brought up in Wiveliscombe and educated at Wellington School, Somerset. By the age of 28 he owned and ran three restaurants in Bristol. He was spotted by a BBC producer and went on to make twenty-six series of television programmes. Floyd was always seen on screen wearing a bow tie and enjoying a tipple or two of wine while preparing and cooking a dish. He worked without a script and was known for barking orders to the cameramen. Floyd also wrote books that combined cookery with travel information. He died suddenly at the home of his partner in Dorset after a meal that included oysters and partridge with champagne.

Frank Foley (1884–1958), who was born in Highbridge, became a spy for MI6. During the Second World War he was sent to Berlin with a cover of being head of passport control.

He used this position to help Jews needing visas to escape persecution. Foley is estimated to have saved the lives of 10,000 people. He is commemorated in Highbridge by a statue that was commissioned by local people.

Shoemaker James Gillingham pioneered the creation and use of artificial limbs in Chard. By 1903 he had treated more than 7,000 patients. Many servicemen who were injured during the two world wars also received limbs made in Chard. James Gillingham died in 1924, leaving his legacy to the world of prosthetics. The firm he founded continued to make artificial limbs until the 1960s.

John Haynes (1939–) is a businessman from Yeovil who made his fortune out of publishing car manuals. He wrote the first one while he was in the Royal Air Force. With a live catalogue of more than 1,700 manuals, his company has a presence in eighty countries and twenty-four languages. In 1985 Haynes founded an international motor museum at Sparkford, near Yeovil.

The comedian and actor Bob Hope (1903–2003), who appeared in more than seventy films, lived in Weston-super-Mare for a short while as a baby. At the time his father was a stonemason who was working on the town's sea wall. In 1908 Hope and his parents went to live in America, where he found fame and fortune as comedian, actor singer and dancer.

Businessman Tom King was elected Member of Parliament for Bridgwater in a by-election in 1970 and represented the constituency for more than three decades. He held some of the most senior offices of state in the government and was a former Defence and Northern Ireland Secretary. King was made a life peer in 2001, taking the title Baron King of Bridgwater. A blue plaque marks his home in Bridgwater's Friarn Street.

Ken Loach (1936–) is a film director who lives in Bath and became famous after directing *Cathy Come Home*, a 1960s television play about homelessness. A poll of Radio Times readers in 1968 voted it the 'best single television drama'. His first feature film, *Poor Cow* (1967) was followed by *Kes* (1969). Ken Loach's television work mainly features social issues.

Artist and academic William Harbutt (1844–1921) was headmaster of Bath School of Art and Design before starting his own art school in the city with his wife. He wanted to provide non-drying clay for his sculpture students so he invented Plasticine. Harbutt started commercial production at a factory in Bathampton in 1900. His descendants later ran the firm and continued to make Plasticine in Bathampton until 1983.

Lord Harding (1897–1989), who had a distinguished military career, was born at South Petherton and went to school at Ilminster. He was a commander of the Desert Rats, an armoured division of the British Army that saw distinguished service during the Second World War, especially in the Western Desert campaign. Lord Harding became Chief of the Imperial General Staff. He lived near Yeovil.

William Herschel, musician and astronomer, discovered the planet Uranus from the garden of his home in New King Street, Bath, in 1781. He used a telescope that he had made in his workshop. Herschel was also a musician and composer, and at one time was Director of Music for Bath.

Edward Higgins (1864–1947) was the third general of the Salvation Army in 1929–34. He was born in Highbridge and followed in the footsteps of his father, who was Commissioner in the Salvation Army and travelled extensively for the organisation. Higgins became an officer when he was 17 years old and spent much of his career with the Salvation Army in the United States. He was the first person who was not a member of the Booth family to lead the organisation, which had been founded by William Booth.

Sir Roger Henry Hollis, KBE, CB (1905–73), who was born at Wells, was a journalist and an intelligence officer who served with MI5 from 1938 to 1965. He held the post of Director General of MI5 in 1956–65. Hollis was a son of a Bishop of Taunton and his wife was the daughter of a canon at Wells Cathedral.

John Keate, who was born at Wells in 1773, the son of a rector of Laverton, became headmaster of Eton College in 1809. When he took over the post, discipline at the school was lax so Keate used birching to restore order and strengthen the authority of the masters. He was headmaster for twenty-five years.

John Lewis (1836–1928), from Shepton Mallet, was the founder of the national department store of the same name. He began his career in the retail trade as an apprentice to a draper in Somerset before moving to London, where he became a silk buyer in a fashion store. In his late teens Lewis opened his own small drapery shop in Oxford Street. The business expanded and in the 1880s the small shop became a department store.

The Macmillan Cancer Relief charity was founded by Douglas Macmillan (1884–1969) who lived in Crewkerne. He was the seventh of eight children and was educated at Sexey's School, Bruton and the Quaker-run Sidcot School at Winscombe. Macmillan, who was a civil servant, became involved in charity work after his father died from cancer.

Deborah Meaden, businesswoman and long-time judge on the TV entrepreneur series *Dragon's Den*, has had a long association with Somerset. She was born in 1959 in the county and lives on a restored farm just outside of Wellington. Meaden has invested more than £1 million into businesses that have been featured on *Dragon's Den*.

Jack Meyer (1906–91) was the founder of one of the country's most prestigious boarding and day schools. He set up Millfield School in the town of Street in 1936 after having taught young princes in the Far East. Meyer established the school on the principles of free choice, self-discipline and a firm religious base.

He developed its reputation by taking all ages and abilities, with the paying pupils' fees subsidising scholarship winners. Millfield School, which is a centre of excellence for sport, brings much kudos to Street. Among the school's former students are Alexander, Crown Prince of Yugoslavia, the actor Jason Connery and singer-songwriter Lily Allen.

Photo-journalist Don McCullin CBE (1935–) lives at Norton St Philip near Bath, where he stayed as an evacuee in the Second World War. The multi-award-winning photographer is best known for the images he has captured from various wars, including those in Vietnam, the Congo, Cyprus and Iraq.

Richard 'Beau' Nash (1674–1762), who was born in Swansea, educated at Oxford and spent some time at London's gambling tables, became Master of Ceremonies in the spa town of Bath. He drew up a code of behaviour for visitors to Bath's public buildings such as the Pump Room and the Assembly Rooms. Royalty and members of the aristocracy became frequent visitors to the city. Beau Nash lived in a grand house next to the theatre with his mistress. He is buried in Bath Abbey.

Beatrice Page from Weston-super-Mare made First World War history when she became the first woman to drive a tram in Britain. As men went off to fight in the war, Page did the same as other women and applied for their jobs. In the case of Weston-super-Mare's tram service, opposition to women drivers was particularly vocal to start with and Page had to hand back her job when the men returned from the war in 1918. However, she was invited to drive the last tram in the town before the tracks were pulled up in 1942.

Suffragette and campaigner Emmeline Pethwick-Lawrence grew up in Weston-super-Mare but moved to London later on to help impoverished working-class women. She became treasurer of the Women's Social and Political Union and came up with the concept for the suffragette colours of green, white and purple, which are still recognised today. Pethwick-Lawrence was imprisoned for trying to make a speech in parliament.

Admiral Arthur Phillip (1738–1814), founder of modern Australia, lived in South Parade, Bath, for many years. In 1787 he was appointed commander of the 'First Fleet' taking convicts to Australia. He arrived there without losing one of them and called the place of settlement Sydney, after the Home Secretary who came up with the idea of a penal colony. Admiral Phillip was the first governor of New South Wales. He is buried at St Nicholas, Church, Bathampton. His second wife, Isabella, who outlived him by a number of years, is buried in the same grave.

Ralph Reader the Broadway and West End theatrical impresario, was the creator of the scout and RAF 'Gang Show', a variety entertainment presented by members of the scouting movement. Reader (1903–82), who was born in Crewkerne, was also known for leading the community singing at the FA Cup Final at Wembley for many years.

William Rees-Mogg (1928–2012), who was editor of *The Times* for fourteen years from 1967, came from an old Somerset family and lived at the Old Rectory, Hinton Blewitt, until he sold it in 1999. His journalistic career began when he joined the *Financial Times* as an assistant editor when he was 24 years old, becoming chief leader writer three years later and then assistant editor.

Haile Selassie (1891–1975) the Emperor of Ethiopia, found his first refuge in a guesthouse at Burnham-on-Sea when he was defeated and exiled by Mussolini in 1936. He later found a more permanent home at Newbridge Hill in Bath, where he lived with his family and staff for five years. Selassie returned to Bath in 1958 to receive the freedom of the city, which was granted to him by the local council.

The inventor of powered flight, John Stringfellow, lived for many years in the High Street of Chard. He was known for the unmanned 10ft-wide monoplane that he built from scratch with wood, silk, and a steam engine that was carried in a container below the fuselage. To avoid disturbance from the wind, Stringfellow conducted the aircraft's first flights in one of Chard's disused lace mills in 1848. The following year he organised a flight in the open air but after being airborne for a distance of 120ft his plane crashed. Stringfellow died in 1883 without much recognition for his invention.

The Rev. Augustus Toplady (1740–79), curate of Blagdon in the Mendip Hills, was a prolific hymn writer. His best-known hymn is probably 'Rock of Ages'. Local tradition has it that the Rev. Toplady wrote it while sheltering from a thunderstorm under a large rock in Burrington Combe, hence the opening lines of his hymn, 'Rock of ages, cleft for me/Let me hide thyself in thee'. The hymn was first published in *The Gospel Magazine* in 1775. A plaque on the cliff marks the spot where Toplady took refuge from the storm.

Hugh Montague Trenchard, who was born in Taunton, was the founder of the Royal Air Force. The 1st Viscount Trenchard was born at Haines Hill in 1873 and spent his childhood in the village of Norton Fitzwarren. He went on to a distinguished military career and in 1918 he became the first Chief of the Air Staff when the Royal Air Force was formed. He is remembered by a memorial in Taunton and the town's northern inner distributor road was formally named Trenchard Way as part of the national RAF 100 celebrations.

Nicholas Wadham and his wife Dorothy were co-founders of Wadham College, Oxford. Nicholas, of Merryfield, near Ilminster, and from a long-established West Country family, died in 1610, leaving funds to endow the college. His widow, who was then 75 years old, was left with the task of buying a site and drawing up the college statutes. She appointed the first warden, fellows and scholars, and even the college cook. Wadham

College was ready to receive its first students – at the time it was a men-only establishment – four years after Nicholas Wadham died. Strangely enough, Dorothy, who added to the endowment from her own resources, never visited Oxford. Nicholas and Dorothy Wadham are buried at Ilminster.

Sir George Williams, who was born on a farm in Dulverton in 1821, was a philanthropist who founded the Young Men's Christian Association (YMCA). This is the oldest and largest youth charity in the world. He started work as an apprentice to a draper in Bridgwater and later moved to a drapery in London. He founded the YMCA in London in 1844 and saw it spread around the world. A stained glass window in Westminster Abbey commemorates Sir George, who died aged 84.

5

SOMERSET SHOW BUSINESS

POP GOES THE FESTIVAL

Farmer Michael Eavis could never have envisaged that the two-day Pilton Pop, Blues and Folk Festival he staged on his Worthy Farm in 1970 would grow into the world-renowned Glastonbury Festival that it has become today. One thousand five hundred people each paid £1 to attend the first festival. Free milk from the local farms was included in the ticket price. In the late 1970s the Bishop of Bath and Wells, the Right Rev. John Bickersteth, persuaded Eavis to allow him to start blessing the festival. Wearing his purple cassock, he addressed thousands of festival-goers, imploring God to bless the event. Over the years the style of the festival programme has changed, facilities improved, and, unsurprisingly, ticket prices increased.

FESTIVAL FACTS

Headline acts at the Glastonbury Festival since it started have included David Bowie, Hawkwind, Ginger Blake, Van Morrison, Elvis Costello, Rod Stewart, Sinead O'Connor, The Smiths and U2.

Michael Eavis made a loss of £1,500 at the first festival.

The event changed its name from Pilton Festival to Glastonbury in 1981. Pilton is a village 6 miles east of Glastonbury with a population of just under 1,000. All the villagers get a free festival ticket.

The year 1981 also saw Glastonbury named as the first Campaign for Nuclear Disarmament Festival (CND). On this occasion £20,000 was raised for CND.

The iconic Pyramid Stage made its debut in 1971 and is now synonymous with the Glastonbury Festival. In 1994, the stage burnt down just over a week before the festival. A temporary main stage was constructed just in time and the event went on as usual.

After torrential downpours that turned the festival site into a quagmire, 1997 has become known as the 'year of the mud'. This has been key to the public perception of Glastonbury Festival ever since.

After years of people gatecrashing the event, festival organisers finally decided to construct a 'super-fence' in 2002, which cost £1 million. Standing at 12ft tall, the barrier is said to be virtually impossible to scale, break through or burrow under.

Michael Eavis joined Stevie Wonder on the Pyramid Stage in 2010 to sing 'Happy Birthday'. He followed that up in 2016, joining Coldplay to sing 'My Way'.

The Rolling Stones made their Glastonbury Festival debut in 2013, appearing on the Pyramid Stage on the Saturday night of the event. The Rolling Stones played twenty songs during their two-hour set, with the second hour broadcast by BBC Two. The group's performance had a peak television audience of 2.6 million.

The power generated during the festival is enough for a city the size of Bath.

More than 4,000 toilets as well as reservoirs holding 2 million litres of water are provided on-site for festival revellers.

The modern Glastonbury Festival is a far cry from the first event. There are now more than 100 stages, 2,000 performers and the BBC broadcasts the event to thirty countries.

The festival site covers 900 acres of farmland that are normally used by Michael Eavis as pasture land for his cows.

Eavis, now in his eighties, ran the festival with his wife Jean until her death in 1999. He now co-organises the event, which runs for five days, with his daughter, Emily Eavis.

There were 544 food stalls and 900 shops on the festival site in 2017.

The festival has grown to become the biggest performing arts festival in the world.

In 2017 Ed Sheeran, Foo Fighters and Radiohead were the headline acts on the Pyramid stage. The festival was a sell-out event with the 135,000 tickets, costing £238 each, all being sold within fifty minutes of the box office opening.

MUSICAL SOMERSET

The hills of Somerset are famous enough to have their own song. It was written by Fred Weatherly of Portishead and called 'The Green Hills O' Somerset'. Weatherly was a barrister as well as one of the most prolific and successful writers of ballad lyrics, having penned some 3,000 of them. His best-known songs include the 'Roses of Picardy', 'The Holy City', 'Up From Somerzet' and the sentimental ballad 'Danny Boy', which was set to the tune 'Londonderry Air' and published in 1913. It has been sung by many well-known recording artists including Bing Crosby, Judy Garland and Elvis Presley. Weatherly, who was born in 1848, died in 1929. At his funeral at Bath Abbey 'Danny Boy' was played as an organ voluntary.

Jimmy Kennedy, who lived near Taunton, was another lyricist. Over fifty years he penned some 2,000 songs, of which some 200 became worldwide hits. Amongst his most popular numbers was 'The Isle of Capri', which he wrote in 1934 and was sung by Gracie Fields. The following year Jimmy Kennedy wrote 'Red Sails In the Sunset', which has been recorded by a number of artists including Nat King Cole, Fats Domino and The Beatles. While he was serving with the Royal Artillery in the Second World War Kennedy wrote the wartime hit, 'We're Going to Hang out the Washing on the Siegfried Line'. Kennedy lived at Staple Grove Elm, which is now a private nursing home. He died in 1984 aged 82 and is buried in the local churchyard.

THE FIRST EVER GLASTONBURY FESTIVAL

Rutland Boughton (1878–1960) was a composer who wanted to stage the equivalent of Germany's Bayreuth Festival in Glastonbury. He began his own event in 1914 that ran each summer until 1926. The first festival included the premiere performance of an opera by Boughton, *The Immortal Hour*. By the time the festivals came to an end, 350 staged works had been performed, as well as a programme of chamber music, lectures and recitals. Financial support for the festivals came from Clarks the shoemakers in nearby Street. Boughton planned five Arthurian music dramas to form a cycle (as in Wagner's *The Ring*), but they were never completed.

WEDMORE OPERA

In 1988 a group of people living in Wedmore on the Somerset Levels gathered around a kitchen table determined to stage Verdi's three-act opera *La Traviata* for two nights in the village hall. Since then every two years or so hundreds of people living in and around Wedmore have worked alongside professional singers, players and designers to create a new production. They have staged works by composers including Bizet, Purcell and Mozart. To mark thirty years of Wedmore Opera in 2018, villagers staged the one-act opera *Cavallaria Rusticana* by Mascagni.

SOMERSET'S OWN OPERA STAR

Susan Chilcott (1963–2003), who lived in Timsbury near Bath, was a soprano, considered by her contemporaries and critics as one of the best of her generation. She had success in many of the world's major opera houses and was particularly known for her interpretations of Britten and Janácek. When she was just 12 years old, Chilcott's talent was noted by singing teacher Mollie Petrie, who remained with her as a singing coach and advisor for the rest of her career. Susan Chilcott died of breast cancer.

FOLK SONG HERO

Cecil James Sharp (1859–1924) was the founding father of the folk-song revival in England in the early twentieth century. He began collecting songs in 1903 when he was visiting his friend – and lyrics editor – Charles Marson in Hambridge, in south Somerset. Eventually, Sharp collected more than 1,600 tunes or texts from scores of singers. He used these songs in his lectures and press campaign to urge the rescue of English folk music. Although he collected songs from other counties, those from Somerset were the core of his experience and theories. He also revived the extinct tradition of English country dance, and in 1911 he set up the English Folk Dance Society.

THEME WRITER

Nigel Hess (1953–) is a composer who has written many theatre and film soundtracks. He also wrote the theme tunes to the television detective series *Maigret* and *Wycliffe*. Hess was born in Weston-super-Mare and was educated at the town's Grammar School for Boys. He went on to study music at Cambridge University and became music director of the university's famous Footlights Revue Company.

A JAZZ LEGEND

Jazz clarinettist Acker Bilk (1929–2014), who came from the coal mining village of Pensford, had the distinction of being the first British artist to have a record at the number one spot in the American Billboard Hot 100. This happened in 1962 with a composition Bilk had written to celebrate the birth of his daughter. However, the BBC chose it as the theme tune for a children's television series, *Stranger on the Shore*. The tune also hit the number one spot of the United Kingdom chart at the same time. At the peak of his career Bilk was playing his clarinet all over the world with his Paramount Jazz Band. He always appeared on stage wearing his trademark bowler hat and striped waistcoat.

THE 'SCRUMPY AND WESTERN' SINGERS

Some of Somerset's villages were put on the musical map when Adge Cutler wrote songs about them for his so-called 'scrumpy and western' band The Wurzels, which he set up in 1966. He gave the songs titles such as 'When the Common Market Comes to Stanton Drew', 'Pill, Pill, I Love Thee Still' and 'Ferry to Glastonbury'. The opening song on Adge's second album was called 'Easton in Gordano' after a north Somerset village of that name.

Unusually for a recording company, EMI moved its bosses and technicians out of its London studios to record Adge Cutler and The Wurzels in the upstairs room of the Royal Oak pub at Nailsea before an invited audience. It was all the more remarkable as the band was newly formed and without any experience of show biz. This pub session in November 1966 saw the first commercial recordings being made by the group. Adge's debut single and the subsequent EP were both taken from the twelve songs that were recorded in the pub.

The group's first record was 'Drink up Thy Zider', which Adge called the 'national anthem of North Zummerset'. More than 100,000 copies of the disc were sold and it entered the British pop charts at number 45. On the other side of the record was another song written by Adge, called 'Twice Daily'. The BBC banned its disc jockeys from playing it, claiming the song was too raunchy.

In 1976, The Wurzels reached the top of the record charts with a song called 'Combine Harvester.' Unfortunately Adge (real name Alan John) Cutler, who was born in Portishead and brought up in nearby Nailsea, had died two years earlier in a car crash. It happened while he was driving home after playing at a concert in Hereford. However, the Wurzels kept together and are still performing at concerts today.

FROM TEACHING TO THE TOP TEN

Former teacher turned folk singer and entertainer Fred Wedlock (1942–2010) shot to national fame at Christmas 1981 with a record called 'The Oldest Swinger in Town'. This was the culmination of years of playing the folk club circuit and happened after presenter Noel Edmonds played the song on a radio programme. The song, which Fred had written himself, soon reached number six in the charts. A string of offers to appear on various radio and television shows, including *Top of the Pops*, followed. Fred, who lived in the hamlet of Timsbury near Bath, was then in greater demand than ever before playing clubs, arts centres and student gatherings at colleges all over the country right up until his death.

INSPIRATION FROM ANCIENT FORT

Solsbury Hill, the site of an Iron Age hill fort, rising 625ft above the village of Batheaston, inspired rock singer Peter Gabriel (1950–) to write a song called Solsbury Hill, which he recorded in 1977. Gabriel was the original lead singer and flautist with the 1970s band Genesis and had his own recording studios at Box near Bath.

PORTISHEAD – THE BAND NOT THE TOWN

Although he originally came from Weston-super-Mare, Geoff Barrow named his trip-hop band Portishead after the town where he spent much of his teens. Portishead, founded in 1991, are often considered one of the pioneers of trip-hop music. Barrow and co-founder singer Beth Gibbons won the

Mercury Music Prize in 1995 for their debut album. He gave the band's first gold disc to Portishead Youth Club, where he once played records, so that it could be auctioned to raise much-needed funds.

ROCK WRITER

The rock musician and song writer P.J. (Polly Jean) Harvey (1969–) was brought up in Yeovil, where she studied art and sculpture at the town's college. Her early music career is said to have been influenced by the bands that she heard in local pubs. Harvey quickly established herself as one of the most individual and influential songwriters of the 1990s, exploring themes of sex, love, and religion with dark humour.

RADIO 1 TAKES TO THE ROAD

Some unexpected fame came the way of the small town of Portishead when local show business agent John Miles and his brother Tony were looking after the merchandising of the BBC's travelling pop show. Each summer weekday for two decades, the Radio 1 Road Show was broadcast live from a different seaside resort. The Miles brothers converted an old furniture van into a mobile stage and studio with all the latest broadcasting equipment for Radio 1's disc jockeys. A second van was turned into a travelling sales shop stocked with promotional items. John said later:

For 21 years from 1972, the name Portishead was hardly off the airwaves. Listeners at home who wanted promotional items such as T-shirts and coffee mugs were told to send their orders to Post Office Box 275, Portishead. Millions of orders came in over the years. There was an amusing side to this because people on their holidays would come to Portishead and ask at the Post Office if they could see the Radio 1 factory. But they were told all box numbers were confidential. The postman brought all the orders to the office at my home, where they were processed by the staff. But it certainly put the name of Portishead on the map.

THE BEATLES (AND OTHER POP STARS) IN SOMERSET

Beatlemania reached Somerset in 1963, when four lads from Liverpool who had formed a rock group called the Beatles were making their first tour of the country's concert halls. Their first stop in Somerset was at the Gaumont Cinema in Taunton on 26 February 1963. The Beatles were a support act for singer Helen Shapiro, who was heading the bill but was unable to appear because of a heavy cold. Her place was taken by Danny Williams, then popular singing 'Moon River', while comedian Dave Allen compered the concert. Taunton's weekly newspaper described the Beatles performance as 'in part, rather amateurish'.

The Beatles were back in Somerset four months later when they performed at the Bath Pavilion. They headed the bill and were supported by local groups Colin Anthony Combo and Chet and the Triumphs. This was the Beatles' only performance in Bath. The admission price was 6s.

Just over a month later, John, Paul, George and Ringo were in the county again – this time at the seaside. They performed a week of concerts at the Odeon Cinema in Weston-super-Mare. The advertising posters described the Beatles, who were topping the bill, as 'Britain's Fabulous Disc Stars!' Also in the concert were Gerry and the Pacemakers. While in Weston, the Beatles made some unreleased recordings with Gerry Marsden of Gerry and the Pacemakers. They were recorded at the Royal Pier Hotel, where the artists were staying.

The Beatles were back at the Gaumont cinema in Taunton in September 1963 doing two shows on the same night. Supporting acts included Freddie Star and the Midnighters, Mike Berry and the Innocents, Ian Crawford and the Boomerangs and Rocky Henry and the Hayseeds. The top price for a ticket was 10s 6d in pre-decimal currency, and that was for a seat in the stalls. Although the venue was a cinema, it had a stage that was large enough – 75ft wide and 21ft deep – to accommodate pop groups, their instruments and sound systems.

The Kinks appeared twice at the Gaumont; first on 30 April 1964 and then on 18 May of the following year.

Taunton's County Ballroom was the venue for two concerts by Queen. The first was on 21 December 1973 and the second on 30 March 1974 as part of their spring tour.

Elton John (later Sir) appeared in Taunton on 30 May 1976 as part of his 'Louder than Concorde' tour.

The Beatles were in Somerset again in 1964 to shoot some of the scenes for their first film, *A Hard Day's Night*, at the West Somerset Railway, which runs from Minehead to Bishop's Lydeard. Three years later the group randomly popped into a fish and chip shop at Roman Road, Taunton, to do some filming for the surreal movie *Magical Mystery Tour*. The shop quickly became packed with the Beatles, actors in the cast and the production crew. Word quickly spread that the Beatles were in town and crowds of teenagers soon flocked to the shop. These scenes never made the final cut of the film, which was shown on BBC1 on Boxing Day 1967.

ROLLING STONES MAKE A ROOFTOP APPEARANCE

A concert by the Rolling Stones band at the Odeon Theatre, Weston-super-Mare, in August 1964 stopped traffic for several minutes. A crowd of teenagers caught sight of the group on the theatre's roof before taking to the stage and surged past a police cordon to get a closer look at their idols. In doing so they held up holiday traffic in the town centre. Lead singer Mick Jagger told the town's weekly paper, the *Weston Mercury*, that he was enjoying himself in the south-west and thought 'it was a very attractive part of the country'.

6

CASTLES, MANSIONS, FOLLIES AND MONUMENTS

AN ENGLISHMAN'S HOME IS HIS CASTLE

Dunster Castle sits dramatically on the top of a wooded hill some 1,100ft above sea level and looks down the High Street of Dunster village. It was originally built to defend Exmoor and the nearby port of Minehead from invaders. The present castle was remodelled in 1868–72 and for 600 years it was the home of the Luttrell family. In 1976 Lt Colonel Walter Luttrell gave the castle, a Grade I listed building, and its parklands to the National Trust. The medieval builders of the castle could hardly have dreamt that seven centuries later their stronghold would help to lead the way in energy conservation. In 2008 Dunster Castle was the first National Trust property to have solar panels installed on its roof, which supply the building with the equivalent of the energy consumed by two family homes in a year.

Farleigh Castle, near Norton St Philip, was built in the fourteenth century by Sir Thomas Hungerford, who was the first Speaker of the House of Commons, as a safe house. His son added to the castle and it remained in the Hungerford family until 1689, when it was sold to repay debts. Since then the castle has had various owners but the crypt of its chapel still houses an unusual collection of human-shaped lead coffins. The remains of Farleigh Castle are now maintained by English Heritage.

Nunney Castle in Nunney village near Frome is often been described as Somerset's finest castle ruin. It was built in the fourteenth century originally as a manor house by Sir John Delamare on the profits of his involvement in the Hundred Years War. During the Civil War the castle was besieged by Cromwell's troops and one of its walls was battered by cannon shot but remarkably it didn't collapse until Christmas Day 1910. Although it's just a ruin, Nunney Castle has become a tourist attraction.

NEW USE FOR A CASTLE

The Great Hall and Inner Ward of Taunton Castle now make up the Museum of Somerset, which tells the story of the county from prehistoric times to the present day. The castle was built in 1107 to defend Taunton and has twice undergone extensive reconstructions – once in the thirteenth century and again in the sixteenth century. It was at Taunton Castle that the pretender to the throne, Perkin Warbeck, who claimed to be one of the princes in the tower, was questioned by King Henry VII. When he was exposed as a fraud the king ordered that Warbeck be hanged in London. The castle was also the principal court for Judge Jeffreys' 'Bloody Assizes' after the Battle of Sedgemoor. In 1874 Somerset Archaeological Society bought the castle, part of which it still uses as a museum, and leased space to Somerset County Museum. It is also the home of Somerset Military Museum.

MANOR HOUSES

Clevedon Court

Clevedon Court, a fourteenth-century manor house on the edge of Clevedon, has been the home of the Elton family since 1709, when it was bought by Abraham Elton I, a wealthy Bristol merchant, one-time mayor of the city and a Member of Parliament. Although there have been many alterations to the house down the centuries, much of the original building is still evident. Friends of the Elton family who visited Clevedon Court include the novelist William Makepeace Thackeray. He wrote parts of his historical novels *Henry Esmond* and *Vanity Fayre* in the house and immortalised Sir Charles Elton's youngest daughter, Jane, as Lady Castlewood. Of the nineteenth-century Eltons, one was a priest, another was a literary man and friend of Tennyson and one, Sir Edmund Elton, was a potter who became known for the pots and vases he made. His work is on show in Clevedon Court, along with glassware from the old glassworks in the nearby town of Nailsea. Sir Arthur Elton transferred Clevedon Court to the National Trust in 1961 but his family still live there and manage it on behalf of the Trust.

Tyntesfield

A Victorian Gothic Revival mansion with forty-three bedrooms and a total of 106 rooms was saved for the nation when the National Trust launched an appeal to buy Tyntesfield at Wraxall in north Somerset. This country house, with its spiralling turrets and pinnacles adorning the roof, was put on the market after the death in 2001 of its owner, the second Lord Wraxall, George Richard Gibbs. He was not married and none of the nineteen beneficiaries in his will could afford to maintain the estate. The National Trust wanted to prevent Tyntesfield from being sold to private interests so it could be opened to the public.

Around £24 million was raised within 100 days as 50,000 individual donors, along with national grant-making bodies, responded to the National Trust's 'Save Tyntesfield' campaign. Within a few months the house was opened to visitors. Tyntesfield was home to four generations of the Gibbs family, and according to the National Trust no one ever threw anything away. Indeed, while the house was being prepared for visitors more than 50,000 items ranging from priceless paintings to ice skates were catalogued by the Trust. Tyntesfield was created on the site of a more modest property in the 1870s by William Gibbs, who made his fortune importing guano – bird droppings – from Peru that were to be used as agricultural fertiliser.

'Bloody Assizes' Reminder

Cothelstone Manor has a grim reminder of Somerset's history. It was here that two of the Duke of Monmouth's followers were hanged by Judge Jeffreys following the Battle of Sedgemoor. It is said that the men met their deaths at Cothelstone Manor after its owner, Lord Stawell, complained about the judge's cruelty in what became known as the 'Bloody Assizes'. Stawell refused to provide accommodation for Judge Jeffreys, who then ordered two prisoners to be hanged on the gateway of the manor. Cothelstone Manor, at the foot of the Quantock Hills, dates back to 1520. It was extensively damaged by Parliamentary forces during the Civil War and for two centuries afterwards was used as a farmhouse before it was restored. It is now used for weddings and corporate events.

Herbalist's Home

Lytes Cary Manor at Somerton was the home of six generations of the Lyte family between the thirteenth and eighteenth centuries. It was here that in 1578 Henry Lyte, a botanist,

published *Lyte's Herbal*, a directory of plants. It was so popular that it was still being printed 100 years later. Over the years the Lyte family gradually expanded the house. After they left Lytes Carey Manor, a series of farmers became tenants. In 1907 the house was bought by Sir Walter Jenner, who found that the Great Hall had been used to press cider apples and the Great Parlour had been a carpenter's workshop. Sir Walter restored the house to a seventeenth-century style and also built a new west wing. He handed the property over to the National Trust in 1948.

An 'Eccentric Electrician's' Home

Fyne Court was the home of Andrew Crosse (1784–1855), whom local people nicknamed as the 'thunder and lightning man' on account of his experiments with electricity. Crosse, a scientist, philosopher and poet, was fascinated by electricity and practised in his garden trying to harness its power during storms. He was born and died at Fyne Court in the hamlet of

Broomfield, and is buried in the local churchyard. In 1894 a fire ripped through the building, leaving most of the property so devastated by the incident that nearly the entire house was pulled down. Historians think the fire started when a housemaid left a candle she'd been using to heat curling tongs unattended. As a result of the fire not much remains of the house in which Crosse lived. The remnants, though, are owned by the National Trust. Fyne Court is now a nature reserve and visitor centre.

Halswell House

Halswell House is mentioned in the Domesday Book of 1086, which says that the lords of the manor were the Halswell family. The main building is now a Tudor manor house, which was built for Robert Halswell, whose son Nicholas became a Member of Parliament for Bridgwater. The architectural historian Nikolaus Pevsner has described the house in the village of Goathurst near Bridgwater as 'the most important house of its date in the county'. It stands in 31 acres of parkland and includes a ballroom, banqueting hall, lake and follies. During the Second World War part of the parkland was used as a camp for Italian prisoners of war.

Forde Abbey

Founded by Cistercian monks 800 years ago, Forde Abbey at Chard became a wealthy monastery. Since the Dissolution of the Monasteries in 1539, Forde Abbey has had a series of private owners. Although it is now a family home, the building still has a monastic air about it. What were once the monks' quarters, refectories and chapter house still play an integral part of the home. Forde Abbey, surrounded by gardens, lakes and ponds, was a setting for a Hollywood film adaptation of Thomas Hardy's novel *Far From the Madding Crowd* starring Carey Mulligan, Michael Sheen and Tom Sturridge.

Ashton Court Mansion

Ashton Court Mansion in the village of Long Ashton on the edge of the county's northern boundary was owned by the Smyth family for more than 400 years. Before John Smyth, a wealthy merchant, bought it in 1545 the house had passed through a number of hands. One owner was granted a royal licence to enclose his house and the land with it with high walls and also to create a deer park, both of which still exist. Various generations of Smyths added cottages and large estates in Long Ashton to their property portfolio, either through purchase or marriage. The most notable feature of the mansion today is the long façade of its south front built in two different styles. When Esme Smyth died in 1946 there were death duties of nearly £1 million to pay. The house and 840 acres of woodland, parkland and gardens were acquired by Bristol City Council in 1960 for £103,200. Although the house, a Grade I listed property, has been used for various functions the cash-strapped council says its future is unclear. English Heritage describes the house as being in 'slow decay'.

Cricket St Thomas

Cricket St Thomas manor house at Chard is probably best known as the location for the 1970 television sitcom series *To the Manor Born*, which starred Penelope Keith and Peter Bowles. The house has fifteenth-century origins but was given a facelift in the early nineteenth century. Frequent visitors were Lord Nelson and Lady Hamilton. The house is now a hotel.

National Trust's First House

Barrington Court at Ilminster was the first major stately home to be acquired by the National Trust in 1907, just twelve years after the organisation was formed. It was bought on the recommendation of one of the Trust's co-founders Canon Hardwicke Rawnsley, a conservationist. The dilapidated state of the sixteenth-century house meant that restoration became a most costly project for the fledgling Trust. However, Colonel Lyle of the Tate and Lyle sugar firm came to the rescue and restored the property. He filled Barrington Court with his collection of interior fittings from contemporary derelict properties.

Barrow Court

Barrow Court in the north Somerset village of Barrow Gurney was a Benedictine nunnery before the Dissolution of the Monasteries by Henry VIII. The property, once owned by the Gibbs family of Tyntesfield, was used as a military hospital in the Second World War. In 1976 the building was turned into residential accommodation.

FOLLIES

A stone arch, about 15ft high and topped by a round stone tower, marks the eastern boundary of Barwick House, near Yeovil, and its parklands. This folly is dedicated to Jack the Treacle Eater. Local legend has long had it that Jack, who used to run to London and Bath and back with messages for local people, used treacle as a kind of eighteenth-century energy drink. The folly dates back to 1775.

Walton Castle at Clevedon, which dates back to the early seventeenth century and stands on the site of an Iron Age hill fort, was never a fortress. It was designed as a hunting lodge for Lord Poulett. It fell into dereliction and has had various owners. It is now a private property. Historic England describes

Walton Castle as 'an unusual castle folly on a very prominent site overlooking the Bristol Channel, for long abandoned and ruined, restructured and again made habitable in the late twentieth century. Most of the work is of this period, but the keep retains some historic value in conjunction with the surrounding curtain walls and towers'.

Wellington Monument, rising up to a height of 175ft on the Blackdown Hills, is said to be the world's tallest triangular obelisk. Originally it was planned for the column to be surmounted by a cast iron statue of the Duke of Wellington with soldiers on the plinth. This rather grand idea of decoration was scrapped because of the cost.

The foundation stone of the monument – it marked Wellington's victory over Napoleon at Waterloo – was laid in 1817. However, it wasn't completed until 1854 because of a lack of both enthusiasm and funds on the part of people living in and around the town of Wellington. The monument, with its spiral staircase of 365 steps, has had a major problem with falling stones. Some funds have been found to repair the top part of the obelisk but the National Trust says that another £3.8 million is needed to restore the whole of it. The Duke of Wellington took the name of the town for his title in 1809, although he had no obvious link with the place. He had only visited it once in his life.

The 'Cider Column'

A 140ft-high Tuscan column standing on Troy Hill at Curry Rivel is officially recognised as the Burton Pynsent Steeple but it is also known by local people as the 'Cider Monument'. The story behind this dates back to the days when Sir William Pynsent, once a Member of Parliament for Taunton, was grateful to William Pitt for opposing a 10*s* tax on a hogshead of cider (1763 Cider Bill), which would have affected his business. Pynsent was so grateful that on his death he left his entire estate to William Pitt. The politician used some of the income from the estate to build the monument to his benefactor. He commissioned the landscape architect Capability Brown to design the pillar, which is clad in Portland Stone. The column was built at a cost of £2,000.

7

LITERARY SOMERSET

The books of Jeffrey Archer, Baron Archer of Weston-super-Mare (1940–) novelist and politician, have sold around 330 million copies worldwide. Educated at Wellington School in Somerset, he became a Member of Parliament in 1969 for five years but did not seek re-election after a financial scandal that left him almost bankrupt. Determined to repay his creditors in full, Archer wrote a novel *Not a Penny More, Not a Penny Less*. He has since written more than twenty fiction titles, three non-fiction books, a number of short stories and three plays. A two-year stint in prison spawned three *Prison Diaries*.

Jane Austen, author of *Pride and Prejudice, Sense and Sensibility, Mansfield Park* and other novels, lived in Bath in 1801–5. Two of her novels, *Northanger Abbey* and *Persuasion*, are largely set in the city. A plaque outside 4 Sydney Place records that she lived there. Although the novelist died 200 years ago 'Jane Austen tourism' is big business in Bath, where there are such events as balls and walking tours named after her.

Richard Doddridge Blackmore (1825–1900) became renowned as the author of *Lorna Doone*. His novel, which is set on Exmoor, first appeared in three-volume form and didn't really become popular until it was published as a single volume. In the novel, Lorna Doone is shot by Carver Doone in the fifteenth-century St Mary's Church, Oare, as she is about to be married. A plaque in the church commemorates Richard Blackmore.

Fanny Burney (1752–1840), who lived in Bath, was a satirical novelist, diarist and playwright. Her most famous novel was *Evelina*, which was set in Bristol. Fanny Burney was a friend of royalty and in 1788 she was appointed keeper of the robes to Queen Charlotte, wife of George III. Fanny Burney, her husband and son are all buried in Bath.

Science fiction writer Sir Arthur C. Clarke (1917–2008) was born in Minehead and educated at Huish's Grammar School, Taunton. He worked in scientific research before turning his hand to writing fiction in 1951. His best known work, *2001: A Space Odyssey*, was filmed by the American director and producer Stanley Kubrick. Clarke wrote nearly 100 books. He moved in the 1950s to Sri Lanka, where he lived for the rest of his life, but occasionally returned to Minehead. On one occasion this was to receive the freedom of the town at a special meeting of the local council in 1992.

The poet Samuel Taylor Coleridge and his wife, Sarah Fricker, honeymooned in Clevedon after their marriage in 1795. They spent two months living in a cottage in Nether Stowey on the west Somerset coast, where they had a visit from the poet William Wordsworth and his sister. While at Nether Stowey, Coleridge wrote some of his best-known poems including 'The Rime of the Ancient Mariner', 'Frost at Midnight', 'This Lime-Tree Bower My Prison' and 'Kubla Khan'. He collaborated with Wordsworth on a volume of poetry called *Lyrical Ballads*. Coleridge and his family left the cottage in Nether Stowey in October 1799. It is owned by The National Trust.

Hartley Coleridge, who was born in a cottage in Clevedon, in 1796 followed in his father's footsteps as a poet. He was also an essayist and teacher. In one of his poems his father describes Hartley as his 'babe so beautiful'.

Charles Dickens visited Bath as a junior newspaper reporter in 1835 when he was working for the *Morning Chronicle*. He was following the progress of the politician Lord John Russell around the country and reporting his speeches. Later, Dickens returned to the city and stayed for two weeks at the Saracens Head pub in Broad Street, where he completed his first big success, *Pickwick Papers*. In this novel Dickens satirises Bath's social life. It's said that during his stay at the Saracens Head, Dickens slept in a chair in the bar, being unable to negotiate the steps to his bedroom – presumably after an evening of quaffing ale.

In 1967 Somerset County Council appointed Robert Dunning, a PhD student at Bristol University, to compile a comprehensive history of Somerset. Forty years later, with only nine of his projected twenty-two volumes completed, Dr Dunning passed the work on to another researcher. Dr Dunning carried out more than 50,000 hours of research, visited 380 churches and chapels, and looked at 200 stately homes. It is said that if his successor continues at the same pace, the project may reach completion around 2050.

The American-born poet, essayist, publisher and dramatist T.S. Eliot (1885–1965) immortalised the village of East Coker, near Yeovil, in one of his *Four Quartets*, a set of four poems. He came to England in 1914, married here and decided to stay. Eliot's ancestors originated from East Coker before they moved to America in the seventeenth century. In 1948 Eliot was granted the Order of Merit by George VI. He was also awarded the Nobel Prize for Literature. Eliot died in London but in accordance with his wishes his ashes were interred in the parish church of St Michael at East Coker. Inside the church there is a plaque in Eliot's memory, which is inscribed with a quotation from 'East Coker': 'In my beginning is my end. In my end is my beginning.' T.S. Eliot's *Old Possum's Book of Practical Cats* was the inspiration for Andrew Lloyd Webber's

1981 musical *Cats*, which was the West End's sixth-longest-running show.

Henry Fielding (1707–54) was a prolific writer who is probably best known for *The History of Tom Jones*, which was published in 1749. Fielding was born at Sharpham Park near Walton on the Somerset Levels, where his father was a shopkeeper. Fielding married a local girl at Charlcombe near Bath in 1734. Sharpham Park is now an organic farm owned by Roger Saul, the founder of the Mulberry fashion label.

Henry Watson Fowler (1858–1933) was a schoolmaster, lexicographer and commentator on the usage of the English language. He is noted for both *A Dictionary of Modern English Usage* and his work on the *Concise Oxford Dictionary*. He was described by *The Times* as 'a lexicographical genius'. Fowler lived in the village of Hinton St George on the edge of Crewkerne, where he died.

Laurence Housman, the playwright, writer and illustrator, moved to Street in 1924, which became his home for thirty-five years. One of his plays, *Victoria Regina*, about Queen Victoria, was staged on Broadway in 1934. Housman was one of seven children, including his older brother, the classical scholar and poet A.E. Housman. He died in 1959.

Elizabeth Goudge (1900–84) was known for her short stories and books for children. She was a best-selling author in both the United Kingdom and America in 1930–60. In 1946 she won the Carnegie Medal for British Children's' books for *The Little White Horse*. Goudge was born in Wells, where her father was head of the city's theological college. In 1936 she wrote the *City of Bells*, in which Wells was disguised as Torminster. In a reported newspaper interview J.K. Rowling, author of the Harry Potter books, said *The Little White Horse* was her favourite book as a child.

Helen Mathers (1853–1920) was the pen name of prolific novelist Helen Reeves, who was born in the village of Misterton near Crewkerne. She achieved acclaim with her debut novel *Comin' Thro' the Rye*, which she wrote in 1875. In some of her books Helen Mathers wrote about her experiences at a boarding school in Chantry near Frome.

Hannah More (1745–1833) was one of the most influential writers and philanthropists of her day. She was also one of the top-earning writers at the time. Her stories for children, plays, religious tracts, a novel, poems and essays are estimated to have given her an income of £40,000. More gradually turned from writing to social reform, fighting poverty and drink. About 1796 she started the first school in Brislington, at the time a village in Somerset but now a suburb in south-east Bristol. In the nineteenth century it was described as 'the most attractive village in Somerset'. Hannah More also founded village schools around the Mendip Hills and worked with the agricultural poor of Somerset. She lived at Cowslip Green near Wrington, where she lies at rest in All Saints churchyard with her sisters.

Elizabeth Singer Rowe (1674–1737) was a novelist and poet who lived in Frome. She wrote mainly religious poetry, but her best known work was *Friendship in Death*, which was published in 1728. The book was a series of imaginary letters from the dead to the living.

One of the leading poets of the First World War, Siegfried Sassoon, is buried in the churchyard of St Andrew's at Mells. In his poetry, Sassoon, who was awarded the Military Cross for his bravery on the Western Front, described the horrors of the trenches. He survived war and wrote a number of semi-autobiographical books. The poet T.S. Eliot described him as the 'most extraordinary of the Great War Poets'. Sassoon lived at Heytesbury, Wiltshire, where he died in 1967 aged 80. He is remembered at Poets' Corner at Westminster Abbey.

Mary Shelley (1797–1851) the second wife of the poet Percy Bysshe Shelley, was just 20 years old when she completed her Gothic novel, *Frankenstein; The Modern Prometheus*. At the time she was living in Bath, firstly in rented rooms in Abbey Churchyard and later in Bond Street. Shelley started writing the book when she was staying on the shores of Lake Geneva. She lived in Bath from September 1816 to March 1817.

The American writer John Steinbeck, probably best known for his Pulitzer prize-winning book, *The Grapes of Wrath*, stayed with his wife in a cottage at Redlynch near Bruton for nine months in 1959. His desk can be seen in Bruton Museum.

Betty Trask was a romantic novelist who lived in Frome and endowed one of the country's main literary prizes. She left a bequest to the Society of Authors to fund prizes for first novels written by authors under the age of 35 in a traditional or romantic, but not experimental, style. The winner receives a prize of £10,000, and the other shortlisted authors receive awards of £5,000 each. The first awards were made in 1984 and are still presented each year. Trask, who lived in a terraced house, wrote thirty-three novels, including the *Merry Belles of Bath*. She died in 1983 at the age of 88. Most of her wealth had been inherited.

Literary success came to Evelyn Waugh (1903–66), a writer and journalist, with the publication in 1928 of his satire *Decline and Fall*. Other works by Waugh include the satirical novel *Scoop* and *Brideshead Revisited*, along with biographies and travel books. Waugh spent the last years of his life in the village of Combe Florey, near Taunton. His son, Auberon, who was born in Dulverton in 1939, was a journalist and contributor to *Private Eye* magazine. He continued living at Combe Florey until his death in 2001.

8

FILM, STAGE, RADIO AND TELEVISION FILE

The cities of Somerset, its coastline and its countryside have long featured in films and television programmes. Way back in 1953 a production crew from Ealing Studios shot *The Titfield Thunderbolt* at various locations around Bath, including a disused colliery at Dunkerton. The village of Combe Hay and the railway between Limpley Stoke and Camerton were also featured, while Monkton Combe station became the fictional Titfield station. *The Titfield Thunderbolt* was a comedy film about a group of villagers trying to keep their branch line operating after British Railways decided to close it.

Wells is a popular location for production crews not only because of its cathedral but also for its unspoilt medieval architecture and narrow streets. In 1972, Vicars' Close was picked as one of the settings for a cinematic adaptation of Chaucer's *The Canterbury Tales*.

In 2002 parts of *The Gathering*, which starred Christina Ricci and Marion Kirkman, were filmed in and around the cathedral and Vicars' Close.

The same locations were featured the following year in the television series *He Knew He Was Right*, an adaptation of an Anthony Trollope novel of that title published in 1869. The film, starring Bill Nighy and David Tennant, follows the breakdown of a young couple's marriage, due to the husband's insecurity.

Among the many television programmes wholly or partly made in and around Wells Cathedral are *Elizabeth R* (2000), *The Six Wives of Henry VIII* (2002), *Doctor Who* (2006), *Flog It!* (2011) *The Hollow Crown: The Wars of the Roses* (2012–16), and *Poldark* (2016).

Vicars' Close was in the spotlight again in 2004 when it was a location for *The Libertine*, a biography of the infamous rebel Earl of Rochester from the seventeenth century. Parts of the film, starring Johnny Depp as John Wilmot, the Earl of Rochester, were also filmed at the Elizabethan Montacute House and gardens near Yeovil.

The City of Wells was transformed into the fictional village of Sandford – although there is a village of that name 14 miles north-west of Wells – for the shooting of the film *Hot Fuzz* in 2006. This was a film about a London policeman, played by Simon Pegg, who was sent to the seemingly quiet village of Sandford. At first life seems dull, but some sinister goings on are soon discovered. As most of the film was shot in Wells, many of its buildings and streets are featured in background shots. However, the cathedral was digitally removed to make Wells look more like a village. The film was directed by Edgar Wright, a former student at the city's Blue School.

Wells Cathedral was taken over in 2006 by a film crew making *Elizabeth: The Golden Age*, starring Australian actress Cate Blanchett in the role of Elizabeth I. The cathedral became Whitehall Palace, while Brean Down, off Weston-super-Mare, was used for a scene in which the queen addresses her troops.

Parts of the film *Pillars of the Earth*, based on a historical novel by Ken Follett about the building of a cathedral, were shot in Wells Cathedral in 2009.

Scenes from Hilary Mantel's Man Booker Prize-winner, *Wolf Hall*, were also filmed in the cathedral and Vicar's Close in 2014.

In the same year, *Galavant*, a television musical comedy starring Vinnie Jones, was filmed for America's ABC studios.

Parts of *The Huntsman: Winter's War*, an American fantasy adventure film based on the Snow White fairy tale, were shot in 2015 in and around Wells Cathedral.

The area of the Market Place in Wells, next to the Crown Hotel, was transformed into St Helier, Jersey, under Nazi occupation in the Second World War for the film *Another Mother's Son* in 2016. It is based on the true story of Louisa Gould, who took in an escaped Russian prisoner of war and hid him as if he were her own. Scenes were also shot at the Parade Gardens in Bath, the village of Priddy on top of the Mendip Hills, and the East Somerset Railway at Shepton Mallet.

Chew Valley Lake and various parts of the Mendip Hills were frequently used by HTV West in 1984–6 for some of the scenes in its popular series *Robin of Sherwood*.

The opening scenes of the first season of the television drama *Broadchurch* were played out along Hill Road, Clevedon. This shopping street became Broadchurch High Street, with a newsagent's shop being transformed into the offices of the *Broadchurch Echo* newspaper. The exterior of a bank was turned into the entrance of a hotel and Clevedon's twelfth-century St Andrew's church in Old Church Road was disguised as Broadchurch's parish church.

Film stars Keira Knightley, Andrew Garfield and Carey Mulligan can be seen treading the boards of Clevedon's restored pier in the romantic drama *Never Let Me Go*, which was made in 2010. The numerous brass plaques that decorate the pier are also symbolic in this film. In reality, the plaques carry the names of people who've made donations towards the pier's restoration and upkeep.

Clevedon Pier was also used by the boy-band One Direction for the shooting of a music video 'You and I' in 2014. In the video band members walk along the pier and turn into each other as they trade lead vocals.

The Grand Pier at Weston-super-Mare and two of the resort's hotels are among locations used for *The Remains of the Day*, filmed in 1992 and starring Anthony Hopkins and Emma Thomson. The film is based on a novel of the same name by Kazuo Ishiguro that was set in 1950s post-war Britain.

The Café, a television sitcom written by and starring Ralf Little and Michelle Terry, was filmed in Weston-super-Mare during the summers of 2011 and 2012.

Some of Bath's best-known Georgian architecture is featured in *The Duchess*, filmed in 2008, starring Keira Knightly. The story is about the life of the Duchess of Devonshire, a fashion icon admired by many in Britain during the eighteenth century. The Royal Crescent was used for her lavish and popular party dances.

Bath's Pulteney Bridge played a big role in the Oscar-winning production *Les Misérables*. It was chosen as the scene for Inspector Javert's dramatic suicide. The water flowing under Pulteney Bridge is, of course, that of the River Avon and not the Seine.

Some scenes of *The Paper Mask*, a medical thriller starring Amanda Donohoe and Paul McGann, were filmed in Cheddar Gorge in 1990.

Filming for a scene in a television series called *Bone Kickers* took place in a field close to Glastonbury Tor in 2008. The story was about an archaeological dig in which an ancient relic was discovered.

Parts of *Pandaemonium*, a film exploring the friendship between the nineteenth-century poets Samuel Taylor Coleridge and William Wordsworth, who both lived in Somerset at one time, was made in 2001. Locations for this costume drama included the Quantock Hills, Nether Stowey, Wookey Hole and Selworthy.

The Belstone Fox, a children's film, was partly shot along the West Somerset Railway track near the village of Crowcombe in 1973. The film chronicled the life of a fox much smarter than the dogs that hunt him.

The Flockton Flyer (1977–8) was a children's television drama series about a preserved railway that was most aptly filmed on the West Somerset Railway two years after it reopened as the longest private railway in England. Parts of *The Land Girls* (1997) starring Anna Friel and Rachel Weisz, were also filmed on the railway, with Crowcombe station disguised as Bamford station.

Parts of the 1988 BBC television series *The Lion, The Witch and The Wardrobe*, based on C.S. Lewis's book, were filmed at Dunster and Cheddar Caves.

CINEMAS PAST AND PRESENT

The Curzon Cinema at Clevedon has been screening films since 1912 and claims to be one of the 'oldest purpose-built continuously operated cinemas in the world'. It was originally called The Picture House. The cinema opened on 20 April with an appeal to help survivors and relatives of the 1,500 people who had lost their lives with the sinking of the *Titanic* five days previously. In 1996 the Curzon Cinema was threatened with closure when it went into administrative receivership. Thanks to support from the local community, it was bought back from the receivers and is now run as a community cinema.

Not only was the Palladium Cinema at Midsomer Norton one of the oldest in Somerset, it was also one of the oldest in the country. It opened in 1913 as The Empire. Two years later its name was changed to Palladium Electric. The last film was screened in 1993. One of the features of the Palladium was its courting – or double – seats in the back row, which were popular with courting couples.

The town of Keynsham lost its Charlton Cinema in 1974, despite a 'Save Our Cinema' petition being signed by 10,000 people. The cinema had opened in 1936.

The Regal Cinema at Wells was built in 1935 in art deco architectural style. It was unusual in that it also had a stage and the building could be used as a theatre. The last film at the Regal was screened in 1993.

The Gaumont Palace Theatre opened as a cinema in Taunton in July 1932. The first film shown was *Sunshine Susie* starring Renate Muller. It was renamed as the Gaumont Cinema in 1937 and closed in 1981.

TREADING THE BOARDS

A Royal First for Bath

The first provincial theatre in the country to be granted a Royal Patent by George III was the Theatre Royal in Bath. It was then in Orchard Street but when the premises proved to be too small the theatre moved to its present site in Beaufort Square. The original theatre became a Catholic chapel where bishops were ordained. It is now a Freemasons' Hall. It was at Bath's Theatre Royal that the young actress Sarah Siddons appeared in plays such as *The Provoked Husband* and *School for Scandal* in 1778 and won the reputation that led to her fame on the London stage.

Two Seaside Theatres

For seventy-six years everything from locally produced opera to variety concerts were staged at the Knightstone Theatre, Weston-super-Mare. The theatre, at the north end of Weston's bay, opened in 1902 as the Pavilion Theatre but its name was changed in 1927. Well-known comedians including Norman Wisdom, Ken Dodd, Morecambe and Wise and Max Miller often topped the bill at the Knightstone, attracting theatre-goers from all over the country. The actress and film star Diana Dors from Swindon also appeared at the Knightstone, as did the 1960s–70s pop star Adam Faith. For many years the local Royal British Legion branch staged its own annual pantomime here. The theatre closed in 1978 following a decline in its popularity.

A fire destroyed Weston-super-Mare's Playhouse Theatre in the High Street at the height of the holiday season in August 1964. The quick actions of a police officer helped the people living above the cinema get to safety, and in the event no one was hurt. The blaze destroyed all but the front and side walls of The Playhouse, both of which were unsafe and had to be subsequently demolished. The local newspapers described the blaze as 'the worst fire in Weston since the Second World War'. The Playhouse was reopened in 1969 with more seats. The curtain went up on a production of the farce *Let Sleeping Wives Lie*, with the actor-manager Brian Rix heading the cast list. The Playhouse still stages productions all year round.

KINGS OF THE THEATRE

John Brodribb, who was born in the village of Keinton Mandeville, near Castle Cary, where his father was a shopkeeper, became a well-known Victorian actor-manager. As such, he was responsible for supervision of sets, lighting, direction and casting, as well as playing the leading roles at the Lyceum Theatre, London, for more than twenty years. During this time he played most of the great Shakespearean roles. In 1895 he was the first ever actor to be knighted. By this time he had changed his name to Henry Irving. He also frequently appeared on the stage at the Theatre Royal, Bath. During his career, Irving played more than 600 roles. He died in 1905 and is buried in Westminster Abbey.

The dramatist and novelist Ben Travers (1886–1980) lived in Burnham-on-Sea, where the spine road running through the Rosewood Estate is named after him. Travers was the writer of such popular farces as *Cuckoo in the Nest* and *Rookery Nook*, which ran for many years at the Aldwych Theatre, London.

Chris Harris (1943–2014) was an actor, writer, mime artist and theatre director who was also an authority on pantomime. He co-wrote pantomimes for the Bristol Theatre Royal and always played the dame. Harris spent his life in Somerset. He was born in Bridgwater and educated at Taunton. He died in Portishead.

Arnold Ridley (1896–1990), who was born in Bath and trained as an actor, was best known for the comedy thriller *The Ghost Train*, which he wrote and appeared in. Ridley served in two world wars and became famous again as Private Godfrey in the television series *Dad's Army*, which ran in the 1960s and '70s.

Sir Cameron Mackintosh, who owns nine London theatres in the heart of the West End, is the first theatre owner in the United Kingdom to become a billionaire. He was also the first British producer to be inducted into Broadway's American Theater Hall of Fame. Sir Cameron was educated at Prior Park College in Bath and lives at Stavordale Priory in Charlton Musgrove, which was built as a priory church in the thirteenth century. It has been a private residence since 1533.

ON THE AIRWAVES

The BBC lost its monopoly on West Country television viewers when independent television arrived in the region for the first time. Television Wales and West (TWW) went on the air, with help from a transmitter on the Mendip Hills, for the first time in 1958, with announcer Bruce Lewis telling viewers: 'We are brim-full of happiness to be on the air.' However, TWW's regional franchise was not renewed by the Independent Television Authority. No reason was given publicly but it was reported that the ITA was not happy that the broadcaster had its headquarters in London, which was seen to be far removed from its viewers in the West Country. When the station stopped broadcasting in March 1968 the last voice to be heard on air was that of the poet John Betjeman with a eulogy. Ironically, it was recorded in a London studio and not one in the West Country.

NEW BROADCASTER ON THE AIR

TWW was succeeded by Harlech Television, a consortium of mainly West Country businessmen backed by some well-known people including actors Richard Burton and his wife Elizabeth Taylor, actor Stanley Baker, broadcaster Wynford Vaughan Thomas and the opera singer Sir Geraint Evans.

Harlech Television started broadcasting in 1968 and a ultra-high frequency transmitter for the West opened on top of the Mendip Hills. In 1970 Harlech changed its name to HTV. At the time a popular theory for the change was that West Country viewers didn't like the Welsh connotation. However, the station was named after its founding chairman Lord Harlech, a politician who was once Britain's ambassador in America. He died in a car accident in 1985.

ITV Down on the Farm

A major annual outside broadcast for HTV was the Royal Bath and West Show at Shepton Mallet, the biggest celebration of rural life in England. It is also the only four-day royal show in the country. It first took place in Taunton in 1852 and then toured the country for more than 100 years before moving onto its permanent site at Shepton Mallet in 1965. Twelve years later the show was given royal patronage. HTV built its own showground studio each year, transmitting special live programmes throughout the day – including its nightly news magazine. The station's main presenters and reporters all decamped from their Bristol studio to Shepton Mallet for the show. Agriculture is at the heart of the Royal Bath and West, and the show usually has 5,000 animals, farmyard machinery from 100 years ago and the latest computerised farm technology on the site. The British Cider Championships and British Cheese Awards have long been popular events here.

HTV lost its on-screen identity in 2004 along with all the other regional independent television broadcasters in the country. They all came under the control of ITV plc. The local station now broadcasts as ITV West Country.

Some Independent Television Personalities

One of TWW's most popular newsreaders in the 1960s was Guy Thomas. It wasn't generally known that he read the news bulletins from a small studio, not much bigger than a broom cupboard, which was behind the main TWW building.

Sally Alford, a doctor's daughter from Weston-super-Mare, joined TWW as a continuity announcer. Another announcer-cum-presenter in the station's early days was Maureen Staffer, who was given an audition just a week before the station went on air.

Alan Taylor started his television career as a continuity announcer with TWW a year after it started broadcasting. He became one of the most popular celebrities, presenting various game shows including *Mr and Mrs*.

Former newspaper journalist Bruce Hockin became ITV's longest-serving regional news presenter when he retired in 1996. He began his television career in the 1960s when he joined TWW as a reporter and later moved over to HTV. Hockin presented the station's nightly news magazine for thirty years, as well as various crime and current affairs programmes.

Richard Wyatt was on the HTV screen for more than twenty years and is probably best remembered as co-presenter with Bruce Hockin of the nightly news programme. He made the headlines himself in the summer of 1976 while filming an item for the forthcoming Weston-super-Mare air show. One of the attractions was to be a 'flour bombing' exhibition with a Piper Cub aircraft dropping bags of flour on a target. Wyatt decided to become the 'target' for his report but unfortunately as the plane was flying at 70 miles an hour a wing dipped, hit his head and knocked him unconscious. Wyatt was taken to hospital but his injuries were not found to be life-threatening. The aircraft had a small dent in the wingtip.

Some BBC Presenters

The BBC's Chief Somerset Correspondent, Clinton Rogers, has always worked in the county as a journalist since leaving school in 1972 and joining the *Wellington Weekly News* as a trainee reporter. After three years, Rogers became a senior reporter on the *Somerset County Gazette* in Taunton. A spell as Taunton district reporter for the *Bristol Evening Post* followed before he joined the BBC in 1982.

Television and radio presenter Ali Vowles, who lives in Bath, began her broadcasting career with BBC Radio Bristol in 1987 on an early morning programme presenting farming news. She can still be heard on the station as well as appearing as a presenter-cum-reporter on BBC television's *Points West* nightly news magazine for the region. However, Vowles has not always worked in broadcasting – one of her first jobs was as a trainee bus driver in Bath.

Rebecca Pow had a career in radio and television that included working for HTV and BBC Radio 4 before she was elected as Member of Parliament for the Taunton Deane constituency. She left television in 2003 to set up a company specialising in public relations for rural matters, farming, food and gardening. Pow was first elected as MP in 2015 and re-elected in the General Election of 2017. In 2018 she won the Climate Coalition's award for being parliament's 'Greenest New MP'.

Anne Diamond, who made her name presenting breakfast programmes for TV-AM and BBC1, began her journalistic career in Somerset as a junior reporter on the *Bridgwater Mercury*. Before that she had a summer holiday job at Butlin's holiday camp at Minehead.

Julia Somerville, who comes from Wells, joined the BBC's radio newsroom in 1972 as a sub-editor. She went on to become a newsreader and reporter for the BBC and ITN.

Broadcaster, programme director and writer Ned Sherrin (1935–2007) was born in Low Ham near Langport. He joined the BBC at the age of 22 and became a producer of the weekly satirical television show *That Was the Week that Was* starring David Frost. He also produced a number of stage shows including *Side By Side* by Sondheim in 1976. Sherrin also presented the popular BBC Radio 4 series *Loose Ends* for a number of years.

BLIZZARDS LAUNCH A RADIO STATION

During the blizzard that hit the south-west of England in 1978 an emergency radio broadcasting centre was set up at County Hall in Taunton. BBC broadcasters kept listeners up to date with changing weather conditions and information about public transport services, along with details of highway closures. Listeners liked what they heard and lobbied for a radio station to serve Somerset permanently.

Ten years later, BBC Somerset Sound was born, going on the air for the first time on 11 April 1988. Its main studios were then based above a café in the town with a smaller station in Yeovil. In November 2017, BBC Somerset moved to a new building on the edge of Taunton in Blackbrook. The local radio service for Somerset has been rebranded as BBC Somerset.

RADIO & TELEVISION PLAYBACK

The television and radio toy museum at Montacute is believed to be the only one of its kind in the country. On display is the largest collection of toys, books, annuals and games relating to radio and television programmes, many of them dating back to the 1960s. There is also a collection of 600 vintage radio and television sets.

9

THE NATURAL WORLD

THE HIGH POINTS OF SOMERSET (AND A LOW ONE)

The hills of Somerset have featured in films, been written about in novels and have even been the subject of songs. The lyricist Fred Weatherly described the hills as 'rolling down to the sea' in 'The Green Hills of Somerset'. The county's principal ranges of hills include the Mendips, the Quantocks, Blackdown Hills, the Brendon Hills and Exmoor.

Dunkery Beacon, on the summit of Dunkery Hill on Exmoor, is 1,705ft above sea level. It is not only the highest point on Exmoor but also in the whole of Somerset. On a clear day there are views across the Bristol Channel to South Wales and down to Dartmoor.

Exmoor has the highest coastline on the British mainland, reaching a height of 1,354ft at Culbone Hill.

The highest point on the Quantock Hills is Wills Neck at 1,261ft above sea level.

The summit of Cothelstone Hill, also on the Quantocks, is 1,089ft above sea level. It was here that the historian John Collinson noted in 1791 'from this delightful spot the eye commands fourteen counties, and with a glass on a clear day 150 churches'.

Blagdon Hill on the Brendon Hills is 1,184ft above sea level.

The highest point on the Blackdown Hills is Staple Hill, which rises to 1,033ft.

Pen Hill near Wells is 1,001ft above sea level. It is home to the Mendip telecommunications and television broadcasting mast, which itself is 922ft high, making it the tallest structure in the south-west.

On the Mendip Hills, Black Down is the highest point at 1,066ft.

Glastonbury Tor is 518ft high. On a clear day people who reach the peak can take advantage of views across to the Welsh mountains.

The highest point on the beauty spot of Brean Down, which juts out 1.5 miles into the Bristol Channel from Weston-super-Mare, rises to 318ft.

The Somerset Levels are one of the lowest and flattest areas in the country. Much of the land is below high water level on spring tides, and has a maximum altitude of only 25ft above sea level.

SPECIAL SITES

Somerset has more than 127 Sites of Special Scientific Interest, ranging from Cheddar Gorge to Langport Cutting. These sites are protected by law to conserve their wildlife or geology. For example, more than 360 botanical species have been identified in Cheddar Gorge and the nearby countryside. One of the biggest areas to be covered by the designation is North Exmoor, where just over 12,000 acres of land are of biological interest.

THE ROYAL FOREST OF EXMOOR

Exmoor National Park came into being on 19 October 1954 when the then Prime Minister, Harold MacMillan, confirmed a Designation Order for the area. It covers an area of 171,189 acres, or 267 square miles, taking in moorland, woodland, farmland and valleys. Exmoor, which was one of the first National Parks in the country, takes its name from the River Exe. In 1993 the government also gave it the status of an Environmentally Sensitive Area.

The River Exe is more than 50 miles long. It rises near the village of Simonsbath on Exmoor and mainly flows due south, so most of the river lies in Devon. It reaches the sea on the south coast.

Exmoor was once one of sixty-seven royal forests where the deer were the preserve of the monarch. The landowners now include the National Trust, which owns more than 10 per cent, the National Park Authority, the Forestry Commission, the Crown Estate and water companies that own land around the reservoirs. The largest private owner is the Badgworthy Land Company, which represents hunting interests.

Hunting of the deer on Exmoor has been going on since Norman times, when the area was declared a royal forest. In the 1870s there were about 1,000 red deer living on the moor. Now the number has risen to about 2,500. This makes Exmoor's herd of red deer the largest in England.

Another of the moorland residents is the Exmoor pony, a horse breed native to the British Isles. Some ponies still roam the moorland as semi-feral livestock, although each one belongs to a distinctive herd. The Exmoor pony, which is mentioned in the Domesday Book, has been given 'endangered' status by the Rare Breeds Survival Trust, and 'threatened' status by The Livestock

Conservancy. Exmoor ponies are always a shade of brown, bay or dun with black points.

'THE BEAST OF EXMOOR'

Since the 1970s, there have been numerous sightings of an alleged 'Beast of Exmoor'. Some people say the animal could be a cougar, while others are adamant it is a black leopard that has escaped from captivity. A report of the 'Beast' seen crossing the road between Exford and Wheddon Cross described it as a black cat but bigger than an Alsatian. Reports of the sighting have taken up much space in local and national papers, with the *Daily Express* offering a reward for the capture of the animal, but to no avail. Farm animal deaths on Exmoor have been sporadically blamed on the 'Beast'. However, the official Exmoor National Park website lists the animal under 'Traditions, Folklore, and Legends'. Meanwhile, the BBC has called it 'the famous-yet-elusive beast of Exmoor'. The Department for Environment, Food and Rural Affairs (Defra) says that 'based on the evidence, Defra does not believe that there are big cats living in the wild in England'.

HILLS OF OUTSTANDING BEAUTY

The Quantock Hills was England's first Area of Outstanding Natural Beauty (AONB), being given the designation in 1956. The Mendip Hills followed with AONB status in 1972 and the Blackdown Hills in 1991. The Quantocks consists of large amounts of heathland, oak woodlands, ancient parklands and agricultural land. It is an area that stretches from the Vale of

Taunton Deane in the south, for about 15 miles to the north-west, ending at Kilve and West Quantoxhead on the coast of the Bristol Channel. About 3,000 people live in the villages on the Quantock Hills.

A NEW HAVEN FOR WILDLIFE

Britain's largest new coastal wetland has been created on the Steart Peninsula, 8 miles from the centre of Bridgwater. Besides being a home and breeding site for everything from birds to dragonflies, the Steart Marshes also help to improve flood management. The saltmarsh and freshwater wetlands act as a buffer for homes and businesses in the local villages from flooding, especially when the tides are higher than usual. Migrating birds have found the site, with 25,000 birds of fifty-one different species being recorded in winter. The saltmarsh is farmed for specialist saltmarsh lamb and beef, and the creeks of the marshland are a nursery for the fry of important fish stocks. The Steart Marshes project is the work of the Wildfowl and Wetlands Trust and the Department of the Environment, Food and Rural Affairs.

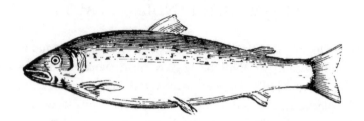

THE SOMERSET LEVELS

The Somerset Levels and Moors is a unique flat landscape that extends for about 170,000 acres across parts of the north and centre of Somerset, stretching from the Mendips in the north to the Blackdown Hills in the south. Thousands of years ago this was an area covered by the sea, but today it is a landscape of rivers and wetlands – artificially drained, irrigated and modified to allow productive farming. The wetlands are supplied by the rivers Axe, Sheppey and Brue in the north, and in the south the rivers Cary, Yeo, Tone and Parrett.

The Somerset Levels are important for landscape, ecology and biodiversity, and contain thirty-two Sites of Special Scientific Interest because of the vast variety of plant and bird species. There are also 72,000 acres designated as Environmentally Sensitive Areas.

Peat extraction on the Somerset Levels dates back to the days when the Romans were in Somerset and it still continues. In modern times it became a commercial enterprise with various firms removing peat – partially decayed remains of organic matter – for selling to the horticultural trade. By 1990 one firm was producing 250,000 tons a year to meet the growing demand, especially from supermarkets and garden centres. However, with increasing environmental concerns about peat extraction, the business now operates on a much-reduced scale.

THE OLDEST KNOWN TRACKWAY

About 6,000 years ago Neolithic people built wooden trackways to cross the wetlands. The oldest man-made trackway was discovered in 1970 on the Shapwick Heath Nature Reserve near Glastonbury. This timber causeway was 6,600ft long and one of a network that crossed the Somerset Levels. Most of the track is still in its original positon, although parts of it have been taken to the British Museum in London and the Museum of Somerset in Taunton. It is known as the Sweet Track – after the man who unearthed it – and is considered by many archaeologists to be one of the oldest engineered roads discovered anywhere in the world. Ray Sweet found it while ditch clearing in 1970.

ON THE WING

Somerset's diverse bird population is said to be declining rapidly. In the past thirty-five years, the number of tawny owls has dropped by 33 per cent, lapwing by 40 per cent, skylark by 52 per cent and house sparrow by 64 per cent.

Two peregrine falcons, which are nesting on the tower of St Mary Magdalene church in Hammett Street, Taunton, are being monitored on closed-circuit camera twenty-four hours a day. The footage has shown that the peregrines have captured thirty-five different species of birds as prey. The peregrine falcon, which can fly at up to 180 miles an hour, is one of the world's fastest birds.

Flocks – or murmurations – of tens of thousands of starlings can be seen swirling in the winter skies above Ham Wall, the Royal Society for the Protection of Birds reserve near Glastonbury. This area on the Somerset Levels is said to be one of the best places in the country to see such large murmurations before the starlings settle down to roost in the Avalon Marshes in the evening. The murmurations are greatest in December and January, as many of the birds have migrated from the colder areas of Northern Europe. During the day the starlings go off to feed.

EBBOR AND CHEDDAR GORGES

There are two gorges in Somerset – the more famous Cheddar Gorge and the lesser known Ebbor Gorge, which has caves where bones of Ice Age mammals were found. A plaque in Ebbor Gorge, near Wookey Hole, says that part of it was given to the National Trust in 1967 by Mrs G.W. Hodgkinson in memory of Winston Churchill. The plaque was unveiled by his granddaughter, Mrs Piers Dixon. The limestone Ebbor Gorge is now managed as a National Nature Reserve. Cheddar's world-famous limestone gorge is 3 miles long and in places is 400ft high. It is both a national site of Special Scientific Interest and an Area of Outstanding Natural Beauty.

Cheddar was once owned by Saxon kings, who built a palace on the land where the Kings of Wessex Academy School now stands. In 1556 Cheddar was bought by Sir John Thynne of Longleat, an ancestor of the present Lord Bath who still owns the caves. The underground caves with their impressive stalactite and stalagmite formations were discovered in the nineteenth century by local men George Cox and Richard Gough.

ABSEILERS ROPED IN FOR CLEAN-UP

The gorge had its first spring clean for many years in the run-up to Easter 2018. A team of fifteen abseilers, calling themselves 'rope access technicians', dangling at the end of a rope 120m above ground spent six weeks removing debris, loose rocks, vegetation, invasive plants and any other detritus that was lying around. The £100,000 project managed by Longleat Estate covered 37,000 square metres of rockface.

'CHEDDAR MAN' DISCOVERED

It was in Gough's Cave that Britain's oldest complete skeleton was buried 9,000 years ago and discovered in 1903 by workmen digging a drainage trench in the cave. The bones were well preserved by the cool limestone surroundings. DNA tests have established that 'Cheddar Man' still has descendants living in the village – just a mile from the cave. This is the oldest virtually complete skeleton that has been unearthed in the British Isles. In an unprecedented examination of the DNA, researchers revealed at the start of 2018 that the first modern Briton had a darker complexion than had been previously thought, along with striking blue eyes, gently curled black hair, wide cheekbones and a delicate chin. Previous reconstructions of 'Cheddar Man', which were not based on DNA data, depicted him with a lighter skin tone. Researchers extracted DNA data from bone powder by drilling a 2mm hole through the skull's inner ear bone. The skeleton of 'Cheddar Man' dates from the time when humans recolonised the West Country after the last Ice Age.

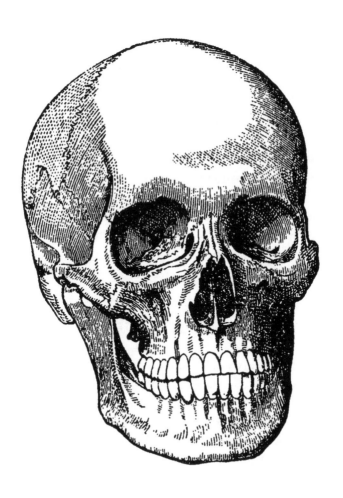

CAVE MUSIC

In November 1892 600 people attended a concert inside Gough's cave amongst the stalactites and stalagmites. It was the first time such an event had been held there. Under the headline of 'Novel Concert', the *Weston-super-Mare Mercury* reported that the cave was lit for the event by 'fairy lamps, Chinese lanterns, gas and candles'.

GORGE TRAGEDY

It was in 1939 that tragedy struck in Cheddar Gorge. A rock weighing about half a ton fell 350ft from the cliff and struck a child standing near the entrance to Gough's cave. Arthur White, who was just 5 years old and lived at Combe Down, Bath, was knocked into the road and killed instantly. He was on a day trip to Cheddar with his family when the accident happened. Other people standing nearby, including Arthur White's mother, were injured by splinters of rock. An inquest into Arthur's death was told that the rock had probably been loosened by rain. A verdict of 'death by misadventure' was recorded at the inquest.

ANCIENT TREES

One of the country's oldest trees, a 3,000-year-old Ashbrittle Yew, stands in the churchyard of St John the Baptist at Ashbrittle. The tree has a circumference of 38ft and is reportedly situated on a Bronze Age mound where a pre-Roman chief is buried. Another yew tree, believed to be 1,000 years old, can be found in the churchyard of St George at Bicknoller.

Known as the 'Domesday Oak', the oldest tree on the 800-acre Ashton Court Estate at Long Ashton in north Somerset is thought to be 700 years old. Supporting timbers and wires hold the trunk together, helping it to survive.

UNDER THE WEATHER

Somerset enjoys a temperate climate. It is generally wetter and milder than the rest of the country. On average the county has 121.2 rainy days and 1,522.7 hours of sunshine per year.

FLOODS DEVASTATE THE WEST

A plaque in All Saints' church, Kingston Seymour, records the day in January 1606 when floodwater inundated the church to a depth of 5ft. It happened when the River Severn breached the sea walls in an area stretching from Gloucester in the north to Glastonbury and Bridgwater in the south. The plaque says that many people were drowned and 'much cattle and goods were lost', and that the 'greatest part (of the water) lay on the ground about ten days'.

LIVES LOST IN 'GREAT FLOOD'

The Summer of 1968
Parts of houses collapsed, stone bridges were washed away, roads became rivers and towns were cut off by flood water after twenty-four hours of continuous rain. The storm devastated scores of communities across Somerset on the night of

10 July 1968. It was centred over Chew Stoke but flooding spread down to the Blackdown Hills and north Devon. The casualty department at Taunton and Somerset Hospital was flooded by 2ft of water. In Taunton, hundreds of homes were awash with flood water and families had to be rescued by boat from bedroom windows. At Burnham-on-Sea the water was 2ft deep in places and further along the west Somerset coast the resort of Minehead was cut off by floodwater.

Lives Lost

A wall of water swept through the Chew Valley, demolishing almost everything in its way. Some properties were beneath 14ft of water and families spent the night on the roofs of their homes waiting to be rescued. At Keynsham a car carrying four people was washed into the River Avon. One of the occupants, a 21-year-old university student, managed to escape in a bid to get help but he himself got into difficulties. He was marooned in a tree for five hours before being rescued by the RAF. Meanwhile his parents and his fiancée, who were in the car, were drowned. The death toll increased during the night as a 70-year-old man at Blackford was killed when he was swept away from his home by flood water, and a man in the village of Pill in north Somerset died while watching the floods.

Chew Valley Badly Hit

In Pensford a 12ft wave swept through the village, demolishing the fronts of several houses. A 100ft-long Army Bailey bridge was speedily thrown across the River Chew by soldiers from the Royal Engineers to replace a centuries-old stone bridge, which was swept away. Nearly seventy bridges in Somerset were either destroyed or extensively damaged.

Cheddar Gorge Blocked

Bulldozers and lorries were called in to clear thousands of tons of mud and rock that blocked the road through Cheddar Gorge. Meanwhile, one farmer in Cheddar lost 40,000 chickens in the flood. As clearing up operations got under way, the Duke of Edinburgh flew into the Chew Valley by helicopter on a morale-boosting trip.

Reservoir's Bonus

Bristol Water Works reported that during the storm its Chew Valley Lake, which serves large parts of Somerset and Bristol with water, gained an extra 471 million gallons of water. The level of the lake rose 19in in less than twelve hours. The storm was said to have been the worst in the area for more than fifty years. National and local newspapers described it as 'The Great Flood'.

SOMERSET WHITE-OUT

Heavy snow fell in the south-west in the middle of February 1978 with blizzards following three days later. Some towns and villages in Exmoor were cut off for several days. Most of Exmoor was covered by up to 2ft of snow, although the worst place was Nettlecombe, below the Brendon Hills, where it was almost 3ft deep.

SEASIDE STORM

A storm in December 1981 hit Burnham-on-Sea, badly damaging the sea wall. It cost the Department of Environment, Food and Rural Affairs £7.5 million to rebuild the current sea defences. It was inaugurated in June 1988. High tides combined with a massive storm surge also resulted in dozens of homes and businesses in the centre of Burnham-on-Sea being flooded.

LAND SWAMPED

People living on the Somerset Levels had their worst winter for years when the area was battered by storms in 2013–14. Some hamlets and villages were under water for nearly three months. Around 30,000 acres of farmland were swamped by about 65 million cubic metres of water. Cattle and horses had to be rescued by the RSPCA. High winds and heavy rain caused power cuts, road closures and widespread travel disruption, with some motorists getting stuck in flood water. Royal Marines from 40 Commando based at Taunton were deployed to help reinforce flood defences. As a major pumping operation got under way, the Prime Minister, David Cameron, said that Somerset's rivers would be dredged once all flood water had drained and river banks were safe.

Prince Charles, who is patron of the Prince's Countryside Fund, visited the Somerset Levels, pledging £50,000 to help people in need. He made his journey around the area by a variety of transport including a boat and sitting on a cart that was pulled through the flood water by a tractor.

DROUGHT

In the summer of 1976 Britain experienced some of the highest temperatures that have been recorded in this country. Parts of Somerset had thirty-eight consecutive rain-free days. The drought brought temperatures of 91°F (33°C). Throughout

August water was being lost in the Mendip reservoirs at an alarming rate – nearly 6 million litres a day – by evaporation. Normally, the reservoir holds enough water when full to supply the region for sixty days before it runs dry. The level in the vast Chew Valley reservoir, which serves large parts of Somerset and Bristol with water, fell so low that people could actually walk on the exposed bed, which had become baked earth. The lake is just over 2 miles long and when full can hold 4,500 million gallons of water.

The *Western Daily Press* reported in 1976 that holidaymakers at Weston-super-Mare and Clevedon were complaining that they were covered in swarms of seven-spotted ladybirds. The drought suddenly ended in the last week of August – after the government had appointed a 'Minister for Drought' – with severe thunderstorms that brought heavy rain and floods.

10

TRADITIONALLY SOMERSET

CARNIVAL COMES TO TOWN

Bridgwater has a reputation in the United Kingdom of being the home of carnival. Each November the streets in the town centre are packed with an estimated 150,000 spectators – some from overseas – to watch the procession of dozens of decorated floats. The parade takes more than two hours to pass any one viewing point on its 2½-mile long route. Each one of the floats known locally as carts – floats were originally built on hay carts or log carts – is illuminated by hundreds of electric light bulbs powered by generators. The fifty or so carts that take part in the procession, accompanied by bands and assorted foot parties, normally use a total of 18,000kW of electricity.

The 'Secret' Floats
Each float is built by one of the many carnival clubs in the town. The design and construction of each one can take up to a year, with all work being done under much secrecy. Designs and themes for the floats are kept under wraps until carnival night. Prizes are awarded in a number of classes ranging from best comic feature float to best decorated towing vehicle. Judges

decide on the evening which floats should be awarded the cups and trophies on offer.

Bridgwater Squibbing

What sets Bridgwater's carnival apart from any other is the squibbing that follows the procession. By definition, squibbing is the simultaneous firing of lots of large fireworks. Carnival organisers claim that it is an event that cannot be seen anywhere else. Around 150 squibbers line the High Street and ignite their squibs as soon as the procession ends. The squib itself is a large firework, strapped to a solid block of wood, which in turn is attached to a large pole. The squibbers hold the squibs at arm's length above their head with the firework facing toward the sky.

The Carnival's Beginnings

The origins of Bridgwater Carnival can be traced back to the Gunpowder Plot of November 1605 when Guy Fawkes and his fellow conspirators failed in their attempt to blow up the Houses of Parliament. Some people say that because Bridgwater was staunchly protestant at the time townsfolk celebrated with greater vigour than anywhere else. Informal bonfire night events were held each year until 1881, when a committee was set up and organised the first 'official' carnival that November. Money collected from carnival spectators is shared between local charities and the carnival itself.

Carnival Towns

Besides the Bridgwater Carnival, similar events are held throughout September, October and November on the streets of a dozen other towns across Somerset: Highbridge and Burnham-on-Sea, Weston-super-Mare, North Petherton, Midsomer

Norton, Shepton Mallet, Wells, Glastonbury, Wellington, Ilminster, Chard and Taunton.

HARVEST HOME

The Harvest Home lunch in the West Country is a tradition that can be traced back well over 100 years. Indeed, the tradition was mentioned in Thomas Hardy's novel *Far From the Madding Crowd*, which was set in nineteenth-century Dorset. This annual event has its roots in the days when farmers put on a meal with cider as a 'thank you' to their farmhands for safely gathering and bringing home the harvest. For many Somerset villages it has now evolved into a day-long event for the whole community at the end of summer. Typical is the Harvest Home at Wedmore, which starts with a church service, followed by a procession through the village led by the Harvest Home King, Queen and Princess. Local organisations and families have colourful trailers drawn through the village by tractors. Lunch in a large marquee on the playing fields ground is followed by sports events for children and then a tea. The day is normally rounded off with a tribute band playing to a packed marquee.

The shopping list for the harvest lunch can include 120lb of cheese, 500lb of roast beef, 100 bowls of salad and an extremely large locally made loaf of bread. Then there is the cider, beer and lemonade. The Harvest Home in many villages lapsed during the Second World War but was revived afterwards.

A FAIR ATTRACTION

St Matthew's Fair at Bridgwater is another tradition steeped in history. It dates back to 1249 and has been held on St Matthew's field each September since the fifteenth century. It was a one-day fair until 1857, when a local act was passed extending it to three days. Poor weather in 1919 resulted in a fourth day being added to help the traders. The fair has run for four days ever since. For many years this was a major agricultural event, with farmers selling horses, ponies and sheep, although one day is now given over to a horse fair. One of the largest travelling funfairs in the south-west is also a major attraction at St Matthew's Fair.

HOBBY HORSE DAY

Minehead is well known for the annual ritual that takes place each May Day. This is when a 'hobby horse', a sign of fertility, begins its journey through this west Somerset seaside town accompanied by drummers, musicians and money collectors called 'Gullivers'. The 'hobby horse' is really an 8ft-long canvas-covered frame carried by masked men, with swinging rope tails.

SHEEP FOR SALE

A sheep fair has been held in the village of Priddy, high up on the Mendip Hills, each August since 1348, when it was moved from Wells because of the plague, known as the Black Death. This is a one-day event that has been known to attract more than 1,000 sheep. Beside farmers, there are livestock dealers and gypsy horse traders. Legend has it that the fair will only survive if a thatched stack of hurdles – kept on the middle of the village green – are preserved. The hurdles are used to form the sheep pens, although some farmers bring their own.

A CRACKING TALE

The rather curious business of egg shackling takes place on Shrove Tuesday every year involving children of the village school at Stoke St Gregory near Taunton. Parents, teachers and the children themselves watch with bated breath as eggs – each one bearing a different child's name – are tossed around in a garden sieve until only one remains unbroken. The name of the child on the shell of the intact egg is added to a special trophy. It's not known for certain how this unusual tradition began but it is thought to date back to 1857 when the school was founded.

WASSAILING

The ancient practice of wassailing takes place in cider apple-growing areas, and Somerset is no exception. This ceremony, which dates back to Pagan times, generally takes place on Twelfth Night, or sometimes on 17 January, known as Old Twelfth. In the apple orchards, toast is soaked in cider (what else?) and placed in the trees for the robins, which legend claims are good spirits. The trees are then dowsed with cider as a blessing to Pomona, the goddess of fruit. As part of the ritual, men fire shots into the boughs of the trees to drive out evil spirits. Special wassail songs are sung and a Wassail Queen is crowned. It's all done, say the cider makers, to ensure a good crop of apples later in the year.

PUNKIE NIGHT

Every year on the last Thursday in October, children living in the village of Hinton St George near Crewkerne take part in a lantern parade known as Punkie Night. Children carrying hollowed-out mangolds or manglewurzels, known as Punkies, with a lit candle inside, are led around the village – there are just 234 properties – by a Punkie King and Queen. The custom is said to date back to the time when the women of Hinton St George, carrying home-made lanterns, made their way around the village in search of their menfolk, who had been to a local fair and were late getting home.

BRIDGE TOLLS CUSTOM

Once a year a group of commissioners gathered around a table at the Langport Arms Hotel with eyes focused on a sandglass. It was part of a ritual to decide who would have 'ownership' for the coming year of Burrowbridge toll bridge on the main Taunton to Wells road. The sandglass was turned after each bid from interested parties. The sand took one minute to run through. When it had been turned three times without a fresh bid, the last bidder became the purchaser. This entitled him or her to possession of a little cottage adjoining the bridge and the right to collect the tolls for the ensuing twelve months from midday on 1 April.

On 1 April 1945 Somerset County Council took on ownership of the toll bridge and this saw the end of toll charges, which had been in place for 120 years. During the total life of the toll more than £24,000 had been paid for the rights. The highest bid was in 1938, when the commissioners received a bid of £1,830. This meant that the owner had to collect 146,000 threepenny tolls before making any profit.

11

FOOD AND DRINK

A TASTE OF SOMERSET

Somerset has a network of more than 8,500 farmers and food producers. The latest figures available from Defra show that total income from farming in the county decreased by 32 per cent between 2012 and 2016 to £345 million. This is compared to 30 per cent for England as a whole.

CHEDDAR STRAWBERRIES

For many years Cheddar was as famous for its strawberries as it was for its cheese and its caves. Commercial strawberry growing dates back to the 1850s, when small baskets of the fruit were sold to visitors. At one time there were more than 200 strawberry growers stretching from Axbridge through Cheddar and into the village of Draycott. Their fields were sheltered under the southern slopes of the Mendip Hills and the mild weather conditions meant that strawberries, with names such as Black Prince, Noble and Leader, cropped from May onwards. Cheddar strawberries were therefore usually the first to reach the shops. In 1960 around 500 tons of strawberries were being sent to markets as far away as Glasgow, Manchester and Leeds. Hotels in London's West End were also putting Cheddar strawberries on their menus.

The 'Strawberry Line'

The Cheddar Valley Railway Line, which ran from Yatton railway station through to Cheddar and Wells, was known as the 'Strawberry Line'. Strawberries were put on trains at these small stations to join the national rail network to be taken to London and other centres. Although strawberries are still grown in the Cheddar area, the crop is nowhere near as big as it once was. In 1963 British Railways closed the 'Strawberry Line' as part of its cuts to the national rail network. However, part of the branch line has been preserved as a cycle track and walkway through fields and orchards. Overseas growers also caused a big dent in Cheddar's strawberry trade as they were getting their fruits into British supermarkets virtually all year round.

CHEDDAR CHEESE

Cheese has been made in Cheddar since medieval times. It was here that a unique method of production was discovered and perfected that resulted in the first authentic Cheddar cheese being made. Today there is only one cheese maker in the village itself. His cheese is made the traditional way by hand, using unpasteurised milk from local cows. The finished product is matured in muslins. Today, Gough's caves in Cheddar Gorge are used as a giant refrigerator as cheeses mature in the low temperatures for about a year.

Despite its name, Cheddar cheese is produced in many countries. The description 'Cheddar cheese' has no protected

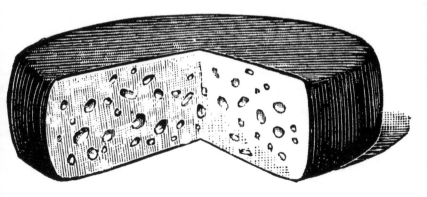

designation of origin within the European Union. However, for a cheese to be described as 'West Country Farmhouse Cheddar' it must be produced from local milk within Somerset, Dorset, Devon and Cornwall and made using traditional methods.

According to Her Majesty's Revenue and Customs data, the value of cheese exports totalled £615 million in 2017. Cheddar cheese makes up for more than 40 per cent of the exports.

Cheese makers were so proud of their product that at West Pennard near Glastonbury a cheese was specially made as a wedding gift for Queen Victoria. It weighed half a ton and was nearly 9ft in diameter. One day's milking of 737 cows was used to make this special gift. The cheese went on show in London but it was found to be inedible and ended up as food for pigs.

Cheeses are still exhibited at all the big farm shows, including the Mid Somerset Show, first held in 1862, and the Frome Agricultural and Cheese Show, which dates back to 1878. There are usually around 1,500 entries in the cheese pavilion each year.

OYSTERS

Oysters, once renowned for their pearls and as an aphrodisiac, are very much on the menu at Porlock once again. The history of oyster fishing at Porlock Bay on the west Somerset coast can be traced back to the 1830s. The industry had a boost in 1874 when the railway reached the area, which meant that oysters put on a train in the morning could be on the tables of top London restaurants that evening. Oyster fishing had become a significant local industry until it suddenly came to an end in the 1890s when a fleet of sailing ship dredgers were in the Bristol Channel and stripped the oyster beds clean.

However, following a two-year pilot that started in 2013, a community-owned business has been formed to farm and sell oysters on a commercially viable basis. More than 100 households in Porlock gave the company loans. At any one time there are up to 750,000 Pacific Bay oysters being farmed. It takes three years for an oyster to grow to a size suitable for the restaurant trade and food outlets. Before it is sold an oyster is moved from a nursery site to spend three months in Porlock Bay. Porlock can lay claim to being the only site in England and Wales to have achieved class A rating for Pacific oyster purity from the Food Standards Agency.

CIDER

Somerset is the county of cider and there are said to be more than 400 different varieties of cider apple grown here; more than enough to keep the keenest 'scrumper' busy. The word 'scrumpy' comes from local dialect and means a small or withered apple. There are said to be thirty-two farms in Somerset devoted specifically to the production of cider apples. Such apples have certain characteristics including high levels of acid, tannin, or sugar, that make them desirable for fermenting into cider.

Cider apples have quaint names including Slack Ma Girdle, Chisel Jersey, Dabinett, Yarlington Mill, Pig's Snout – because of its resemblance to a pig's nose – Cider Lady's Finger, Foxwhelp and Kingston Black. The latter is so named as it was first grown in orchards around the parish of Kingston St Mary near Taunton, where the inhabitants refer to it simply as the 'black apple'.

Cider making has progressed a long way from the days when it was turned out in farmyard sheds. State-of-the art equipment is now used by cider makers using computer-controlled presses.

It is now a multi-million pound industry with people from Land's End to John o' Groats partaking of a glass or two of cider, which used to be a regional drink.

Taunton has long been associated with cider making. In the eighteenth century the Rev. Thomas Cornish planted his orchards at a rectory at Norton Fitzwarren on the edge of the town. This cider had a reputation of being some of the finest produced in the West Country. Its reputation is said to have spread to St James's Palace, London, where the young Queen Victoria had it on her shopping list. In 1911 Norton Fitzwarren became the home of a large-scale cider-making mill. A century later, following changes in the cider industry, Taunton Cider Company effectively disappeared until it was re-registered in 2015 by a group of cider enthusiasts. The first bottles of the reborn company rolled off its cider presses in November 2016.

A NEW BREWERY

The village of Butcombe in north Somerset has been well known for brewing beer of the same name since 1978, when Simon Whitmore set up his own business. He had been a former managing director with Courage Western Brewery and started Butcombe Brewery with his redundancy payment. He used it to convert an old stone barn and outbuildings at his Georgian home into a brewery and buy the necessary brewing equipment. Initially, Mr Whitmore was producing around twenty barrels of beer a week and delivering them to his customers himself. Butcombe Brewery is now under new ownership and has moved to Wrington (just a few miles from its original home). It now has thirty-five pubs on its estate across the south-west, with seven of them in Somerset.

'I'D LOVE A BABYCHAM'

In 1953 Francis Showering, a brewer in Shepton Mallet, began marketing a drink called Babycham. This was a sparkling champagne perry, which was served in a champagne glass. It was a drink aimed specifically at the female market and became very popular in the 1960s and '70s. The creation of Babycham was backed up with an extensive television and newspaper advertising campaign using a chamois deer logo and a catch phrase: 'Just say I'd love a Babycham.' When it first came on the market the drink was selling at 1*s* 3*d* a bottle. Mr Showering's firm had been making champagne perry since 1750. His family were big benefactors to the people of Shepton Mallet. Among their gifts to the town were a multi-purpose theatre and conference centre and homes for the elderly.

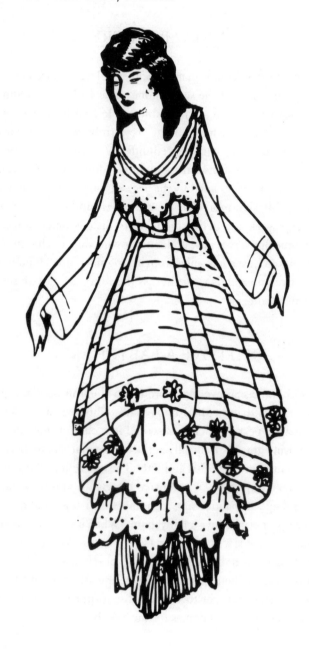

SOMERSET PUBS WITH TALES TO TELL

The 200-year-old Tucker's Grave pub, situated at a crossroads on the A366 Wells Road, between Faulkland and Norton St Philip, is named after a Mr Edward Tucker, a farmworker, who committed suicide in a nearby barn in 1747. He was buried at the crossroads. People who committed suicide were not at the time allowed to be buried in hallowed ground, but were to be interred in unmarked graves, usually at a crossroads, supposedly so the soul would be confused and not find its way to Heaven. In September 1827, the building was originally granted its full license to sell 'bread and other victuals, beer, ale and other liquors'. The story of Edward Tucker and Tucker's Grave has been immortalised in a song by The Stranglers rock group, which featured on their 2004 album *Norfolk Coast*. Tucker's Grave is Grade II listed and is featured in the National Inventory of Historic Pub interiors, which is maintained by the Campaign for Real Ale.

The 300-year-old Drum and Monkey at Kenn, Clevedon, attracted a large crowd of local dignitaries, including the High Sheriff of Somerset, the local chaplain and magistrates. The occasion was the public execution in 1830 of three men who had set fire to local haystacks. Before the execution the public officials assembled in the Drum and Monkey and then made their way to a temporary gallows that had been set up. William Wall, John Rowley and Richard Clarke were the last Englishmen to be hanged at the scene of their crime. The Drum and Monkey is said to be haunted by the ghost of a previous landlady who was known as Nellie No Change.

The name of the fourteenth-century Black Horse at Clapton in Gordano in the Gordano Valley is believed to come from the pit ponies and horses that hauled coal to Portishead for shipping. The pit was at the end of the pub's garden. Around this time the lounge bar of the Black Horse, which is nicknamed the Kicker, doubled as the village lock-up and the window is still barred today.

One of Glastonbury's oldest buildings is the George and Pilgrims Hotel, in the High Street, which has been providing a place of rest for pilgrims and quenching their thirsts for more than 500 years. With its stone frontage, mullion windows and old oak beams, this is said to be one of the oldest purpose-built public houses in the south-west.

The Ship Inn at Porlock on the west Somerset coast dates back to the thirteenth century. In 1798, Robert Southey, who later became Poet Laureate, wrote a sonnet while imbibing at the Ship's bar. It begins 'Porlock, thy verdant vale so fair to sight …'

At more than 700 years old, the George Inn at Norton St Philip is certainly one of Somerset's, if not one of England's, oldest public houses. Indeed, it was first licensed as an ale house in 1397. It is thought that the George was purpose-built by Carthusian monks to accommodate merchants and traders travelling to Norton St Philip for the annual wool fairs. Many well-known people have either slept under the George's oak-beamed ceilings or eaten here. The diarist Samuel Pepys dined here in 1668 and the Duke of Monmouth spent a night at the George before the Battle of Sedgemoor. The architectural historian Nikolaus Pevsner has described the pub as 'one of the most remarkable inns in England'.

Historic England announced in May 2018 that it had chosen a post-war public house at Twerton in Bath to be granted Grade II Listed Building status. The Centurion features a large bronze figure of a Roman centurion on its exterior and a statue of Julius Caesar in the lounge bar. Announcing the listing, Historic England said that it was 'a fascinating post-war pub' and that it was 'embedded in English culture'.

LAST ORDERS FOR BREWERIES

The Oakhill Brewery in Oakhill village near Shepton Mallet, which was founded in 1761, became well known for its Oakhill Invalid Stout. At the start of the twentieth century the brewery was producing up to 2,500 barrels of it a week. With production booming, the firm built its own narrow gauge railway to transport the barrels to the Somerset and Dorset Railway at nearby Binegar. Two locomotives, *The Mendip* and *The Oakhill*, were used to pull the goods wagons. After a fire caused extensive damage to the main building, Oakhill Brewery was acquired by George's and Company of Bristol, which was steadily absorbing many of its competitors.

The Wiveliscombe Brewery was set up in 1807 and gradually became a major source of employment in the area. In 1927 it merged with the Rowbarton Brewery, which was founded in Taunton in 1876. The new combined business was itself taken over in 1955 by Ushers Brewery in Wiltshire. The breweries in Wiveliscombe and Taunton were subsequently closed.

The Lodway Brewery, owned by Hall and Sons in the north Somerset village of Pill, lost its independence in 1912 and came under the banner of George's and Company in Bristol.

The Charlton Brewery at Shepton Mallet produced its first barrels of beer in 1886. In 1937 it was taken over by Bristol United Breweries, who themselves became a subsidiary of George's in 1952. Nine years later the national brewer Courage Barclay & Co. acquired George's.

12

THE WORKING LIFE – PAST AND PRESENT

EVERY VILLAGER A MINER

Lead has been mined on the Mendips since at least the Roman period and St Cuthbert's and Chewton Lead Mines in Priddy were operated from at least the early sixteenth century. Their final phase began in the mid-nineteenth century, when improvements in waste processing meant it was more economical to re-work the waste left by earlier mining activity.

Many people living in the Mendip villages depended on mining for their living. Typical was the village of Shipham where there were more than 100 lead and calamine mines. The historian John Collinson wrote in his *History of Somerset* published in 1791:

> The number of houses which comprise this parish is seventy-three, the habitants are about 380, and almost all of them miners. There are upwards of one hundred of these mines now working, many of which are in the street, in the yards, and some in the very homes. The usual depth of these shafts is from six to twelve fathoms.

WORKING UNDERGROUND

The Somerset Coalfield

Stroll across many a field in north Somerset and you will be treading on the top of what was a dark and dangerous workplace for hundreds of men and boys. Underground is a honeycomb of disused coal mines. In some parts of the area mining is believed to date back to Roman times. By the end of the eighteenth century 1,500 men and boys were working in the pits in the Radstock area alone. Coal mining was once one of Somerset's biggest industries. This coalfield was part of a larger one that stretched from Cromhall in south Gloucestershire to the slopes of the Mendip Hills in the south and from Bath across to Nailsea in the west.

Pit Accidents

Falls of rock were the most common form of accidents in the pits but explosions in the confined working conditions were not unknown. Wellsway pit suffered one of the most devastating disasters in 1839 when twelve men lost their lives. It happened when a rope lowering the men into the pit snapped. At Norton Hill, ten miners were killed in an explosion in 1908. Amongst those who lost their lives was a 14-year-old boy who had just left school to work in the colliery. The other nineteen men working in the Norton Hill pit at the time were rescued. Seven miners and four horses were killed in an explosion at Upper Conygre Pit at Timsbury in 1895. The explosion occurred during the night shift of 6 February. The funeral of five of the miners took place at a joint service at St Mary's church in Timsbury. A Miners' Memorial Garden in Timsbury commemorates the men. The coal pit was being worked from 1791 to 1916.

End of the Mines

The Somerset coalfield reached its peak production by the 1920s. The Writhlington Coal Company ran the majority of the mines in the Radstock area, including the Radstock and Kilmersdon pits, which were said to be amongst the most financially viable in north Somerset. The pits that survived until 1947 became part of the National Coal Board. However, the expense of improving equipment and working conditions meant that even these pits became uneconomical to run and were gradually closed. Kilmersdon Colliery was the last to shut in March 1973, putting 425 miners out of work.

Memories of the Mines

Most of the surface buildings of the pits have been removed, and apart from a winding wheel outside Radstock Museum, little evidence of their former existence remains. One of the features of the museum is a reconstructed candle-lit coal mine. Local people wanted to recognise the work of the Somerset miners and their contribution to Britain's heritage. The result of this foresight is an extensive collection of artefacts from Somerset's coal-mining history.

SIX FIRMS '100 NOT OUT'

Many well-known high street businesses have failed since the 2008 recession and the following period of austerity. Others have been swallowed up by international conglomerates, while some others have celebrated their 100th anniversary with descendants of the founding fathers still at the helm.

In 1833 Daniel Barber began making cheese on his farm near Shepton Mallet. Nearly two centuries later his descendants are still there making cheese and say they are the oldest surviving cheddar cheese makers in the world. Originally milk from their cows was sold locally and the cheese was made for the Barber family and workers on their Maryland Farm. Over six generations, land has steadily been added and the dairy herds have grown accordingly. Two thousand Holstein Friesian cows in turn produce a substantial amount of the milk required for cheese making.

People working for the family firm of Dawson Steeplejacks certainly need a head for heights as they are likely to be climbing some of the tallest buildings in the land. The firm, based at Hewish near Weston-super-Mare, was founded in 1837 in Yorkshire. However, the family moved to the south-west to build chimneys for Cornwall's tin mines. Once these were completed, Dawson's moved its headquarters to Somerset, where it built chimneys for coal mines. The firm is best known now for repairing spires and towers of parish churches and cathedrals

all over the country, as well as restoring weather vanes. The fourth, fifth and sixth generations of the Dawson family are now working together in the firm.

William Thatcher made his first apple cider at Myrtle Farm in 1904. At the time the drink was being given to farmhands as part of their wages. More than a century later, some 4 million pints of cider leave the Thatcher farm at Sandford, at the base of the Mendip Hills, each year for clubs, pubs and retailers all over the country and even overseas. Myrtle Farm was originally a working animal farm and it was only in 1984 that the last of the pigs were taken to market so the family firm could concentrate more on making cider and provide space for more orchards.

The small market town of Frome is home to one of England's longest-established high street jewellers. As a business, Charles Hart has been trading in one form or another since the early part of the nineteenth century. The jewellery business is still owned by descendants of the original family and has been trading in Frome since 1898. It now occupies premises in a medieval street in the town centre.

The world-famous Clarks shoe firm was founded by Cyrus Clark in 1825 when he started tanning sheepskins to make rugs. Three years later his brother James joined him and they started making slippers, later adding boots and shoes to their production line. In 1842 Clarks sold 12,000 pairs of shoes. The family firm has always kept its headquarters in the town of Street, although it moved its shoe-making operation overseas for a while for

economic reasons. The empty shoe factories were turned into the first shopping outlet centre in England with around 100 high street retailers, restaurants and cafes. Clarks Village now attracts 3½ million visitors a year. In 2017 Clarks announced a return to shoe production in Street. The firm says it will build a robot-assisted factory in the town designed to make around 300,000 pairs of desert boots each year.

Sheepskin jackets, slippers, rugs, gloves and footwear have taken the name of Glastonbury all over the world through the export business of Morlands. It was in 1875 that John Morland bought a tannery in Glastonbury, an area that he said had water of 'unusual purity'. This was an essential element in the tanning process. John Morland was chairman of the company from the day he founded it until his death in 1934 at the age of 96. During the Second World War the firm made flying jackets and boots for the RAF pilots who fought in the Battle of Britain. The company was a family business for over 100 years before running into difficulties in the recession of the 1980s. The large tannery closed and the manufacturing process was moved to a smaller building.

A BANK FOR SOMERSET

One of the last privately owned banks in England and Wales was that run by Fox, Fowler and Company, which was founded in Wellington in 1787. It issued its own banknotes, which it was legally entitled to do, until it was bought out by Lloyds Bank in 1921. By the time of the takeover, Fox's Bank had expanded to fifty-six branches in Somerset and Devon. It capitalised on the crash of the West of England and South Wales Bank in Bristol in 1878, which had a total of forty-seven branches, taking up much of its business. The Fox Fowler bank was run as a supplementary business to the family's main activity of wool making.

THE PILL HOBBLERS

The Pill Hobblers are known to have existed from at least the seventeenth century. They still provide the linesmen who handle the lines for all shipping passing through the locks and onto the quaysides at Royal Portbury and Avonmouth Docks. The hobblers are responsible for mooring the ships. Traditionally, they have always lived in the north Somerset village of Pill, which gives them easy access twenty-four hours a day to the nearby Avonmouth and Royal Portbury Docks.

ROPEWORKS REBORN

Rope and twine making were significant industries in Somerset in the nineteenth century, with between thirty and forty manufacturers known to have operated. The introduction of steam power led to production taking place in covered walks, rather than in the open. Coker Rope and Sail Trust has been granted £400,000 by the Heritage Lottery Fund to restore Dawes Twineworks in West Coker near Yeovil, which is almost certainly the last surviving twine works with its original Victorian machinery. Its machinery and fittings represents all stages of the manufacture and finishing of twine and Coker sailcloth. The Dawes worksite was built in 1895 on the site of an earlier twine works but it closed in 1968. The Coker Rope and Sail Trust has been given a 125-year lease on the site and plans to bring Dawes back to life. Flax and hemp industries, such as twine, rope and sailcloth, flourished in the Age of Sail. Coker canvas, as it was known, was the Royal Navy's premium sailcloth.

TRADING NAMES & TRADES SOMERSET HAS LOST

Butler and Tanner, Book Printers

When William Langford, a chemist in Frome, set up a printing business in 1845 it was for his own use. He was able to print his own medicine labels and leaflets about new pharmaceutical products. When he went into partnership with a friend Langford printed Frome's first almanac. As the printing business grew

there were various management changes at the top and the firm became known as Butler and Tanner. It was soon getting a name for printing books for many leading publishers. Very often well-known authors would turn up at the factory to see their books come off the printing presses, providing a photo opportunity for newspapers and television programmes. However, Butler and Tanner ran into financial problems and eventually closed in 2014.

Purnell's of Paulton, Printers

Paulton was one of the villages where for many years coal mining provided the main occupation. However, with the closure of village pits, printing took over this role. In 1839 Charles Dando Purnell set up a printing business in Paulton, along with print shops in nearby Radstock and Midsomer Norton. From printing bills, books and postcards, his firm went on to win orders to print the Bible. Sometimes the compositors would have to set the text in Norwegian and Swahili. Not only did Purnell's of Paulton become a byword in printing but also one of Europe's biggest printers, employing 2,000 people in its heyday. In 1964 Purnell's merged to form the British Printing Corporation. The Paulton factory was still working until 2005 when it closed with the loss of 400 jobs

Nailsea Crown Glass

For many years the skyline of Nailsea was dominated by the cones of its glass factory. Nailsea Crown Glass and Glass Bottle Manufacturers was founded by John Robert Lucas in 1788 and became one of the largest glass factories in the country. About 300 people were employed making glass for windows along with bottles for the brewing industry. The factory closed in 1873. Much of the site now lies under a supermarket car park.

Fry's chocolate

Thousands of chocolate bars with names such as Aero, Bounty, Crunchie, Kit Kat and Tiffin rolled off the production lines at Fry's factory at Keynsham for the best part of a century. One of its best-known brands was the 'Five Boys' chocolate bar, probably because of the design on the wrapper. This had five pictures of a boy's face in various states of emotion. The pictures were titled Desperation, Pacification, Expectation, Acclamation and Realisation. Joseph Fry founded his chocolate company in Bristol in 1756 but when it merged with rival firm Cadbury, its seven factories in the city were gradually closed. When Fry's moved onto the Cadbury green field site at Somerdale, Keynsham, it continued to trade under its own family name. Most of the firm's staff were women and known as 'Fry's Angels'. The management expected them to be 'teetotal, Christian, punctual and clean'. In 2009 Cadbury's announced that it would be closing the factory and transferring production to Poland. Around 400 people lost their jobs. The site of the chocolate factory at Somerdale has since been developed into residential accommodation officially known as the Chocolate Quarter.

Mustad Ltd

Nails for horseshoes were made at Portishead from 1911, when the Mustad firm of Norway built a factory in the town. It was the only such factory in this country and ran until the 1980s, giving work to hundreds of people. Mustad's were so proud of their process of making the nails that staff were sworn to secrecy about it.

Lacemaking

Lacemaking dominated Chard's industrial scene from the 1820s onwards, with the product being exported worldwide. One of its purpose-built lace mills was that of Bowden's, which is now a listed building. Another one was Holyrood Lace Mill, which made plain net from 1829 to 1964. The lace industry had a setback in 1842 when hundreds of mill workers walked out following a cut in their wages. This led to angry scenes and the Mayor of Chard called out the Ilminster Yeomanry. After the strike ended the Yeomanry withdrew but they were followed by an angry mob throwing stones. Lacemaking continued in the town into the middle of the twentieth century, when the last mill in Chard shut its doors for the last time.

A HANDY JOB

Glove making has been the dominant industry in the Yeovil area for many years. In the nineteenth century this was a flourishing business with many women collecting the necessary materials from the factories to make the gloves at home. However, there was a setback for the industry in the middle of the 1820s when the law banning the entry into this country of overseas-made gloves was lifted. It led to the *Sherborne and Taunton Journal* reporting on 21 May 1829:

> The situation of our neighbouring poor who used to find employment in the glove manufactory in the town of Yeovil and all the adjoining districts, is, we regret to say, very distressing; and when we look at the extent of the importation of foreign gloves, we see little prospect of any improvement. The quantity imported this year to the end of the month of April is 24,813 dozen, which would have given employment for 100 days to 1,000 women and children for the sewing, and a proportionate number of men and boys in the dressing and preparing the leather.

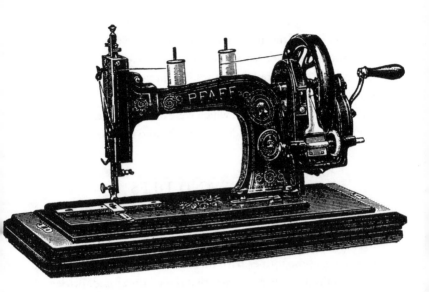

Just before the outbreak of the Second World War there were as many as fifty firms in the Yeovil district making gloves. After the war many of them closed because of cheap imports.

THE BRICK THAT CLEANED

Bath Brick cleaning pads were not made in Bath, as the name might suggest, but in Bridgwater. Although it was one of the town's best-known products, it's not clear how the name came about. At one time there were around a dozen factories making the brick, sited mainly along the banks of the River Parrett. Between them they turned out some 24 million bricks – so-called because of their shape – a year. The Bath brick was a predecessor of the scouring pad and it was said to be suitable for cleaning and polishing metalwork and cutlery without causing any damage. One of the manufacturers, Hunt and Robins, advertised that bricks would be 'carefully packed in boxes for export'. The bricks were also popular with soldiers in the British Army. Bath bricks were made from a mixture of alumina and silica particles with clay, lime and sulphur, which were dug out of the river bank, left to weather, then moulded into shape and dried out in a kiln.

BRICKS AND TILES

One of the main attractions at Bridgwater's Brick and Tile Museum is the only remaining tile kiln in the town. It used to be one of six at the former Barham Brothers Yard at East Quay. It was last fired in 1965, the year that the works closed. Brick and tile making were two of Bridgwater's labour-intensive industries. At one time there were sixteen brickyards along the River Parrett, on both sides of Bridgwater's town bridge, giving work to around 1,300 people. Bridgwater exported bricks and tiles to many countries including France, North Africa and America.

RISE AND FALL OF A PACKAGING FACTORY

One of Bridgwater's biggest employers in the twentieth century was British Cellophane. The company started making the packaging material in Bridgwater in 1935 when it built a new factory covering almost 60 acres on the former Sydenham Manor Fields. In 1940 the firm turned to helping the 'war effort' by producing munitions and Bailey bridges ready for the pending invasion of Europe. Cellophane production was resumed after the war and by the late 1970s the firm was employing more than 3,000 people and producing 40,000 tons of cellophane each year. As sales dropped with the introduction of alternative packaging materials the factory closed in 2005.

WORK IN PROGRESS

What is believed to be one of the biggest civil engineering projects in European history is now going ahead on the west Somerset coast. The £19.6 billion Hinkley Point C nuclear reactor will provide low-carbon electricity for around 6 million homes. The development is set to generate £100 million a year in the local economy and will create more than 25,000 jobs during peak construction. The power station is being built on a headland on the Bristol Channel coast 5 miles north of Bridgwater. It will be dominated by two other power stations – Hinkley Point A, which started generating electricity in the 1960s, ceasing production in 2000, and Hinkley B, a gas-cooled reactor that was commissioned in 1976. Excavations carried out by archaeologists in preparation for the construction of Hinkley Point C discovered a farming settlement at the site dating from the Iron Age, and then a post-Roman cemetery.

FLYING HIGH

One of south Somerset's largest employers is the helicopter manufacturer now known as Leonardo, but still often referred to as Westland's, which has been on the same site at Yeovil since the 1930s. Westland's lay claim to designing and building the first aircraft to fly over the summit of the world's highest mountain, Mount Everest, in 1933. Besides designing and building helicopters for the military, Leonardo also build them for commercial use.

WATER, WATER, EVERYWHERE

A major construction job in the 1950s was the building of Chew Valley Lake. Over five years, thousands of workmen ranging from pipe layers to clay puddlers – workmen who line ponds and reservoirs with puddle clay – were involved. To make way for the reservoir the ancient hamlet of Moreton, which was mentioned in the Domesday Book, was destroyed. It meant that sixteen farmhouses and eleven other residential properties fell into the mouth of the bulldozer, along with 5,000 trees and 70 miles of hedges. The lake was created by damming the River Chew and submerging farmland in the Chew Valley. The Queen, accompanied by the Duke of Edinburgh, officially opened Chew Valley Reservoir on 17 April 1956.

SUCCESS STORIES

The Bilbie family of Chew Stoke were renowned as bell-founders. Between 1698 and 1812 they cast and hung 1,350 bells at church towers all over the West Country. Edward Bilbie's first and oldest surviving bell, cast in 1698, is still giving good service at St Andrew's church in Chew Stoke today. The family is remembered by Bilbie Road in Chew Stoke.

Roger Saul, with £500 backing from his mother, formed the luxury fashion accessories firm Mulberry in 1971. The brand's first pieces were handmade in the family home and the first Mulberry collection was sold from a stall at London's Portobello Road market. In 1973 Roger Saul opened a factory in the village of Chilcompton near Bath. At the time about 450 people were on the payroll. A second factory has since been opened at Bridgwater. It was formally named The Willows after the sculpture of the Willow Man that overlooks the

M5 motorway nearby. Mulberry continues to make designer leather goods at its original factory, known as The Rookery. Altogether Mulberry now employs 1,400 people, half of them in the two Somerset factories. The firm now has stores throughout the United Kingdom and in various parts of the world, including Europe, America, Australia and Asia.

Sir Fred Pontin launched his holiday camp empire at Brean Sands near Burnham-on-Sea on the Somerset coastline in 1946. He set it up in a former military camp that had been occupied by American forces involved in the planning of the D-Day Normandy landings. Although he didn't have the £23,000 himself to buy the site, Pontin raised the money from a variety of sources, including the bank and contacts he had made while working as a stockbroking clerk before the war. Within a year Pontin had set up six holiday camps across the country, catering for a total of 1,300 holidaymakers. He died a millionaire aged 93. Although the business he founded has been taken over a number of times, the camp at Brean is still welcoming holidaymakers.

West Somerset's economy was given a major boost when Sir Billy Butlin built a holiday camp at Minehead. It was constructed on 165 acres of former grazing marshes and cost £2 million to build. The site had been selected because of its flatness, good rail links, and its closeness to both the town centre at Minehead and the sea. The camp, which is still running, opened in May 1962. Although it has had several large refurbishments, many of the original buildings, including most of the chalets, still remain. Status Quo played some of their early concerts at Minehead and returned in 1990 to perform a twenty-fifth anniversary concert.

From making his first brass candlestick in 1848, James William Singer went on to start a business that became known in many parts of the world for its iron work, church ornaments and statues. The firm had export orders from as far away as Australia, New Zealand, India and South Africa. It displayed its goods at exhibitions in London and Paris in the 1860s and 1870s. J.W. Singer & Sons is responsible for casting many of London's famous statues, including that of Justice on the Old Bailey and Boadicea on the Thames Embankment. The completion of a statue by the firm was often a cause for local celebration. The people of Frome would line the streets to watch teams of horses pull the finished work through the town to the railway station. Then they would cheer and clap and throw their caps in the air as the train moved off. The site of Singer's original factory is now a housing development. The firm, much reduced in size, is now on a trading estate on the edge of Frome making brass sprinkler frames for the fire prevention industry.

13

LAW AND ORDER

HOW THE COUNTY WAS POLICED

The Municipal Corporations Act of 1835 introduced the idea of professional police forces. Before then law and order was upheld in a variety of ways, including unpaid watchmen, parish constables and magistrates. In 1856 the County and Borough Police Act made it obligatory for counties to establish police forces. Before then there were various forces throughout Somerset.

'Strong Men' Needed for Bath Police

Bath City Constabulary was formed in 1836. As part of the recruitment process, Bath Corporation displayed a notice seeking potential policemen outside The Guildhall. It stated that all applicants should be between 25 and 34 years of age, and that they should be able to read and write and they must be taller than 5ft 7in without shoes on. All candidates were also required to be 'strong and free of bodily complaint'.

The Formation of Rural Forces

Chard Borough Police Force had just two officers when it was founded in 1839. One of them also acted as the town crier. Chard Police merged with the Somerset Constabulary in 1889.

The town of Bridgwater set up its own Borough Police Force in 1839, which later merged with Somerset Constabulary.

Somerset Police Force came into being on 1 September 1856. The 260-strong constabulary was based at Taunton. Its first chief constable was Valentine Goold, aged 43, one of nineteen people who applied for the job. Mr Goold was previously a sub-inspector in the Irish Constabulary. A chief constable's salary was set at £600 inclusive of expenses.

The Somerset and Bath Constabularies joined forces in 1967. The chief constable of the amalgamated force was Kenneth Steele, who lived in the village of West Monkton, near Taunton.

There were further changes in the policing of a large part of the West Country when the Avon and Somerset Constabulary was formed in 1974. This came about from the amalgamation of Bristol Constabulary, the Staple Hill Division of Gloucestershire Constabulary and the Bath and Somerset force. Today, the Avon and Somerset force serves a population of nearly 1.6 million people across 1,855 square miles. Its 'patch' takes in cities, seaside resorts, market towns, farms, villages, moorland and forests.

Since the Avon and Somerset force came into existence it has had eleven chief constables, albeit three of them were acting chief constables holding the post while the recruitment process was under way to find a permanent incumbent. The force's first chief officer was Kenneth Steele. He retired in 1979.

In 2016 Andy Marsh was appointed to the top job, returning to the force he joined as a recruit in 1987. He went on to be chief constable for Hampshire and the Isle of Wight. Mr Marsh was awarded the Queen's Police Medal in 2018 for his 'dedication to the role'.

NEW HQ FOR NEW FORCE

In the 1990s Avon and Somerset Police moved from their headquarters in the centre of Bristol into purpose-built offices at Portishead in north Somerset. The new headquarters cost £41 million and was built on a 47-acre site. On the site are various operational departments and administrative functions ranging from criminal investigations and the road policing unit, to purchasing and supply departments. When the queen officially opened the new building she was presented with a truncheon made of Bristol Blue Glass.

BOW STREET RUNNERS

Barrister and writer Henry Fielding – probably best known for his novel *Tom Jones* – along with his half-brother John, are credited with co-founding London's first police force, the Bow Street Runners. Henry, who lived at Sharpham Park near Glastonbury, recruited 300 Runners, who were based at his office in Bow Street. The organisation was formed in 1749 but disbanded ninety years later.

ENGLAND'S OLDEST GAOL

England's oldest civilian prison, until it closed in 2013, was in Shepton Mallet, just south of the Mendip Hills. It opened in 1610 and when it closed the prison was a Category C Lifer Prison able to hold 189 prisoners. The building itself is Grade II* listed. During the Napoleonic War, Shepton Mallet prison housed French prisoners of war. In the Second World War,

Cell 10 was used to protect some of the nation's treasures, including the Domesday Book, a copy of the Magna Carta and the logs of Nelson's Flagship, HMS *Victory*.

Shepton Mallet prison became the place of execution for the county of Somerset from 1889, having taken over from Taunton, and civilian executions took place there up to 1926. There were seven judicial executions between 1889 and 1926. On 2 March 1926 the last civilian execution took place when Tom Pierrepoint hanged John Lincoln for a murder in Wiltshire. During the Second World War Shepton Mallet jail was adopted as a military prison by the British and Americans. By the end of 1944, sixteen American soldiers had been hanged and two shot by firing squad for crimes that included rape and murder.

FOOD PRICES CAUSE RIOTS

In 1867 rioting over the prices of meat and bread became widespread, affecting Street, Shepton Mallet, Chard, Ilminster, Frome, Castle Cary and Bruton. In Frome, 200 special constables were sworn in to support fifty regular officers in dealing with a mob of 3,000. The situation was resolved by the bakers reducing their prices – so rioting was not likely to have been seen as a fruitless exercise. It seems that the tradesmen of Ilminster did not take similar avoiding action and became targets of the mob there. A petition on 11 December 1867 for recompense under Riot Damage law was summarily dismissed by the Justices.

SMUGGLING

The Old Chantry at Kilve, west Somerset, was once a religious site built by a brotherhood of monks in 1329. Some years after the brotherhood disbanded, the building became a store for smugglers bringing in contraband goods under the cover of darkness. It was mainly used for storing smuggled whisky. Some parts of the building were badly damaged by a fire in 1848, which was thought to have been caused by an attempt to destroy casks of brandy before customs officers could seize them.

FROM THE CRIME RECORDS

A temporary gibbet was erected at Bincombe on the Quantock Hills in 1789 for the hanging of John Walford, a charcoal

burner, who had been convicted at court of killing his bride of three weeks in what was described as 'a most gruesome manner'. The body of Jane Walford had been found at the roadside on a Sunday morning. Her husband had beaten his wife and cut her throat while she was returning from the Castle of Comfort pub in the early hours. After his trial at the Assize Courts, John Walford was hung on the gibbet and his corpse was left to swing for a year and a day, hopefully to deter other people from committing crime.

On 27 May 1825 five prisoners were executed at the 'new drop' at Ilchester Prison after they had been sentenced to death by a judge at the Somerset Assizes. Samuel Blanning and Henry York were convicted of highway robbery; Phineas Radford had been found guilty of sheep stealing; John Gill and John Willmott were both convicted of horse stealing. The oldest of the men was 28 years of age.

A hamper, apparently containing wine, was dropped off at the George Inn in March 1829 for the purpose of being put on a stagecoach heading for London. One man in the pub, thinking that the straw in the hamper appeared to be very loose, put his hand into the bottom of the basket and felt the feet of a human body. The hamper was immediately opened and found to contain the body of a woman. It was subsequently discovered that a grave in Cannington churchyard, near Bridgwater, had been opened a few days previously and a body exhumed. Newspapers reported that several people were taken into police custody on suspicion of being concerned in the affair. However, the man who delivered the hamper to the pub had absconded.

James Clase, aged 52, was executed at Ilchester Prison in May 1827 having apparently confessed at Somerset Assizes to stealing no fewer than 100 horses. William Hewlett, aged 23, who was found guilty of having stolen seven ewe sheep, a total of eighteen lambs and five hog sheep from various owners, was also executed.

One local newspaper carried a report in December 1916 about the activities of a gang of turnip thieves in Somerset. It said:

A banditti of turnip stealers, forty in number, attacked and cruelly beat on the 10th inst. the four sons of Mr Symes, a farmer, of Yeovil, who, with five others, were stationed to protect a turnip field from their depredations. The Captain of the gang gave the word 'Close your files, attack, attack!' but although two of the farmer's party were so much beaten that their lives are in danger, they succeeded in repelling the plunderers, and securing three of them, who are committed to Ilchester gaol for trial.

SOME UNUSUAL INQUESTS

During the nineteenth century coroners travelled all around Somerset holding inquests into sudden deaths. Instead of having a permanent court building, as is the case today, the coroner very often carried out inquests in public houses, hotels and even private homes.

In January 1825 it was reported that Mr Caines, a coroner from Langport, held an inquest into the unusual circumstances regarding the death of a Mr Collier, a chandler of Keynsham. He was on his return home when he was drowned in the river near his house. At the inquest it was supposed that the horse got out of his depth in attempting to drink.

In July 1825 Mr Caines was at Evercreech to conduct an inquest on John Ridout, who was discovered in a lime kiln 'completely roasted'. It was supposed that he went on the kiln to sleep, in ordered to be in readiness to proceed to the coal pit early the next morning, and must have rolled in. A verdict of accidental death was recorded.

In October 1825 Mr Caines held an inquest into the death at High Ham of Thomas Farrow, aged 42 years. The coroner heard that the deceased who, while in a cider house (being subject to fits) fell into a vat of apple juice, and was found drowned. A verdict of accidental death was recorded.

In March 1827 an inquest was held at the Crown and Sceptre in Taunton on the body of a Mr Hawkes, a labourer who worked on the Taunton and Bridgwater Canal. His body was discovered floating in the canal near Fire-pool Weir. It was supposed that the wind blew his hat off, and that in endeavouring to regain it, he fell in, and was drowned. A verdict of accidental death was recorded.

14

MILITARY MATTERS

HERE AND NOW

Somerset has long-standing links with the armed forces, particularly the major units based in the county such as the Royal Naval Air Station at Yeovilton and Norton Manor Camp at Norton Fitzwarren on the outskirts of Taunton, where 40 Commando has been based since 1983. When 40 Commando was formed in 1942 it was the first Royal Marine commando unit. This battalion-sized Royal Marine unit within 3 Commando Brigade has seen front-line service in Afghanistan on Operation Herrick in 2012. On that tour of duty some 650 personnel were committed to the Nahr-e Sarah district of Helmand Province. Previous deployments were in the Sangin region of Helmand Province.

When men from 40 Commando returned from their tour of duty in Iraq in 2003 they brought back an unusual souvenir – an 8ft statue of Saddam Hussein. The 2-tonne solid brass sculpture was found when the unit was fighting in a town near Basra. It was similar to one that had been torn down by US forces in Baghdad, symbolising the end of Saddam's reign. The commandos gave the statue a new home in the officers' mess at Norton Manor Camp.

Somerset is also home to Royal Naval Air Station Yeovilton, which is one of the Royal Navy's two principal air bases in the country. It is one of the busiest military airfields in the United Kingdom. Yeovilton is home to more than 100 aircraft operated in both front-line squadrons and training units, including the Fleet Air Arm Wildcat Force and the Commando Helicopter Force.

Yeovilton also hosts the world famous Fleet Air Arm Museum, which has most of the planes used by the service over the last 100 years including the Swordfish, Sea Fury and Sea Vampire, on show. One of the museum's exhibition halls is the retirement home of Concorde 002, the first supersonic aircraft assembled in Britain. This was a prototype Concorde, which made its maiden flight in 1969 from the British Aircraft Corporation's factory at Filton, on the northern edge of Bristol, to RAF Fairford, Gloucestershire. After seven years of extensive supersonic testing, Concorde 002 made its last flight to the Fleet Air Arm Museum in 1976. The aircraft had made 438 flights (836 hours), of which 196 were supersonic.

THE BATTLE OF SEDGEMOOR

Westonzoyland near Bridgwater was the scene of the last pitched battle fought on English soil. As was the custom of the day, the battle happened at a pre-arranged time and place. The Battle of Sedgemoor was fought on 6 July 1685, starting between 1 and 2 o'clock in the morning. This was the final battle of what was known as the Monmouth Rebellion. It followed a series of skirmishes around south-west England between the forces of James, 1st Duke of Monmouth and troops loyal to James II. It was an attempt by the Duke of Monmouth to seize the English crown from his uncle, the Catholic King James II. Victory went to the government. After the battle, the duke was taken to London and executed for treason on Tower Hill.

St Mary's church, just south of the battlefield, took on an unusual role as a prison immediately after the fighting stopped. Some 500 of the rebels, many of them wounded, were packed into the church for the rest of the night. Gibbets were erected outside St Mary's and some of the men were hanged the next day.

THE 'BLOODY ASSIZE'

Many of Monmouth's supporters were tried by Judge Jeffreys, who was the Lord Chief Justice, in what became known as the 'Bloody Assize'. Judge Jeffreys held courts in various parts of the south-west, including Taunton and Wells. In Taunton the cases were heard in the Great Hall of Taunton Castle (now the home of the Museum of Somerset and Somerset Military Museum). A total of 514 people went on trial here. Nineteen of the convicted rebels were hanged, drawn and quartered in the centre of the town, at the Cornhill, now known as the Parade. At Wells a makeshift court, shut in by wooden screens, was set up in the space under the Market Hall.

CREATION OF SOMERSET LIGHT INFANTRY

After the Monmouth Rebellion, James II gave orders for a number of foot regiments to be raised across the country. One of them was the Somerset Light Infantry, which was created in 1685. It was a light infantry regiment of the British Army and served under various titles until 1959. It was then amalgamated with the Duke of Cornwall's Light Infantry to form the Somerset and Cornwall Light Infantry. Since then several more military shake-ups have been announced by the Ministry of Defence and the Light Infantry is now part of The Rifles.

A ROYAL SNUB

It is often said that following the Battle of Sedgemoor no member of the royal family visited Somerset for 300 years. Reputedly, Queen Victoria was so ashamed by events in the county that when her train passed through Somerset she pulled the curtain down on her carriage window.

WAR HEROES

The people of Bridgwater have no reason to forget one of their town's most famous sons. A museum, a street and pleasure gardens are named after him. There's also a life-size statue of Admiral Robert Blake (1598–1657) who was twice Bridgwater's Member of Parliament. He became famous for his defence of Bristol, Lyme Regis and Taunton during the Civil War. Blake was made admiral and defeated Prince Rupert's fleet. He distinguished himself in the Dutch War, and destroyed the fleet of Barbary pirates off Tunisia. A statue of Admiral Blake, which stands at the top of Fore Street, has an inscription on its plinth stating that he died at sea.

John Chard VC (1847–97) was one of eleven men who were awarded the Victoria Cross in 1879 for the defence of Rorke's Drift against 3,000 Zulus with a small British garrison. The Victoria Cross is the highest military decoration for valour 'in the face of the enemy' that can be awarded to members of the British armed forces. Chard earned the decoration for commanding a small British garrison of 139 soldiers that successfully repulsed an assault by some 3,000 to 4,000 Zulu warriors. He died in Hatch Beauchamp near Taunton. Rorke's Drift was recreated in the film *Zulu*, in which Chard was portrayed by the actor Stanley Baker.

Harry Patch (1898–2009), who was born in Combe Down, Bath, had the distinction of being the last surviving solder known to have fought in the trenches on the Western Front in the First World War. He was conscripted in October 1916, and by June 1917, aged just 19 years, found himself on the Front at Passchendaele, serving as a lance corporal with the Duke of Cornwall's Light Infantry and operating a Lewis gun. He was struck in the groin by a piece of shrapnel, which was removed without anaesthetic. Patch was invalided home but was not demobilised until the end of the war, although he never returned to the trenches. After the war he returned to work as a plumber. Patch died at a nursing home in Wells five weeks after his 111th birthday and is buried at Monkton Combe near other members of his family.

THE 'THANKFUL' VILLAGES

During the First World War the Somerset Light Infantry suffered nearly 5,000 casualties. War memorials were erected in most of the county's towns and villages. However, nine villages in Somerset are known as the 'Thankful Villages'. These are the villages where all the men who went to fight in the First World War returned home.

The villages have been identified as Aisholt, Chantry (near Frome), Chelwood (near Bath), Holywell Lake (a hamlet in Thorne St Margaret near Wellington), Rodney Stoke near Cheddar, Shapwick, Stocklinch, Tellisford and Woolley. The villages of Stocklinch and Woolley have double reason to be thankful as they didn't lose any soldiers in either the First or the Second World War. No other county in England has as many 'Thankful Villages' as Somerset.

LEST WE FORGET

Memorials by Lutyens

Churches are known for their memorials to the dead, many of them taking the form of plaques. However, St Andrew's church at Mells, a rural village on the Mendips, has an equestrian statue inside the church in memory of a villager. Mounted on a horse and wearing military uniform is a sculpture of Edward Homer, who was wounded and subsequently died in the Battle of Cambrai in 1917 in the First World War. Homer, a 29-year-old lieutenant with the 18th Hussars, came from the family who held the manor of Mells. His statue is by the horse painter Sir Alfred Munnings, while the plinth on which it stands was designed by the nationally renowned architect Sir Edwin Lutyens. He also designed the Cenotaph in Whitehall, amongst many other memorials.

Another of his works in Mells is the village war memorial. This is a column topped with a figure of St George slaying a dragon. The memorial was funded by public subscription and was unveiled in 1921 to honour the twenty-one men from Mells who lost their lives in the First World War. Their names are inscribed on panels at the foot of the column. Another inscription says: 'We died in a strange land facing the dark cloud of war, and this stone was raised to us in the home of our delight.' Extra panels were fixed to the memorial after the Second World War to commemorate those who lost their lives in that conflict. Lutyens was friendly with two prominent families in Mells and it's believed that this led to him receiving several commissions for buildings and structures in the village.

PAULTON REMBERS AIR CRASH VICTIMS

Twenty-one paratroopers and two pilots lost their lives when their aircraft crashed on its way to the Battle of Arnhem in 1944. As the glider flew over the village of Farrington Gurney there was an explosion on board, which resulted in the aircraft splitting in two and crashing in the Double Hills meadow at Paulton. Twenty-one sappers from the 9th Field Company (Airborne), Royal Engineers, and two pilots from the Glider Pilot Regiment, 1st Airborne Division were killed. A memorial has been erected on the crash site and each September families of the victims, war veterans and serving military personnel gather for a commemoration ceremony and parade.

RAF AIRFIELDS

A number of Royal Air Force airfields that were based around Somerset played a vital part in the Second World War. Probably the best known, because of its long and continuing naval tradition, was the Royal Naval Air Station at Yeovilton.

Some RAF Stations and their Locations
RAF Westonzoyland, near Bridgwater, was set up in the early 1920s and is one of the country's oldest military airfields.

RAF Charmy Down, near Bath, opened in 1941. It was initially a base for night fighters trying to intercept raiders on Bath and Bristol. In 1943 the airfield was used by the United States Army Air Force. Charmy Down was decommissioned in 1946 and the remains of the base are now on private property, being used as agricultural fields.

RAF Merryfield is in the village of Ilton near Ilminster.

Tragedy struck the airfield in November 1945 when a Liberator aircraft carrying soldiers to India failed to clear the top of the Blackdown Hills in thick fog. The aircraft came down, killing all twenty-five people on board. RAF Merryfield is now a Royal Naval Air Station serving as a satellite to the much larger RNAS Yeovilton. It is used mainly as a training facility for helicopter pilots.

RAF Culmhead, with its three tarmac runways, was in Churchstanton on the Blackdown Hills.

RAF Lulsgate Bottom was in operation for six years until 1946. After it was abandoned by the RAF, the site became the home of the Bristol Gliding Club. In 1949 and 1950, the Bristol Motor Cycle and Light Car Club hosted motor races on a 2-mile circuit but due to planning and noise issues the club moved in 1950 to a site in Wiltshire. Bristol City Council bought the former airfield in 1955 to develop the site into Bristol Airport. The airport's name may be a misnomer as it is 7 miles south of the city and well and truly in Somerset.

FORTS IN THE BRISTOL CHANNEL

Brean Down Barracks
On the headland of Brean Down, an outcrop of the Mendip Hills that juts out 1.5 miles into the Bristol Channel, the government built a Palmerston Fort in the 1860s. It was named after Prime Minister Lord Palmerston and was designed to provide protection for the Bristol Channel ports against a possible Napoleonic invasion. The fort was built 60ft above sea level, was equipped with seven guns and occupied by twenty soldiers. However, no shots were ever fired in action but regular drill and gunnery practice was part of the routine for soldiers.

An explosion wrecked the Brean Down fort in 1900, killing one gunner and injuring another soldier. It happened in the early hours of 4 July after a gunner by the name of Haines fired a carbine into an ammunition store containing 5,000lb of gunpowder. An inquest into the death of gunner Haines heard that he was 'temporarily insane' at the time.

After the explosion the fort was decommissioned but it was brought back into use in the Second World War for experimental weapons testing. The barracks, which are 9 miles south of Weston-super-Mare, have been restored and opened to the public by the National Trust.

Steep Holm Fort

Six miles out into the waters of the Bristol Channel off the coast of Weston-super-Mare is the tiny island of Steep Holm. In Victorian times it was an army garrison but that was abandoned in 1898. The island was again put back to military use in both the world wars. In 1915 admiralty coastguards were stationed on the island and in the Second World War army engineers installed four large battleship guns, a rocket launcher and huts to accommodate soldiers.

THE DECOY TOWNS

Black Down, the highest point on the Mendip Hills, played an unusual role in trying to protect Bristol from enemy action in the Second World War. At 1,068ft above sea level, Black Down was chosen as a site for a bombing decoy town. Burning bales of straw soaked in creosote were used to give the effects of incendiary bombs already dropped by bomber aircraft. Glow boxes were used to simulate the streets and railways of Bristol. Drums of oil were also set on fire to give the impression of a town already on fire following an earlier wave of bomber aircraft. Decoy towns were part of Operation Starfish, a scheme designed to protect major towns and cities across the country. In the event, Bristol was one of the most heavily bombed cities in the country during the Second World War.

WAR WORK

From Statues to Munitions
At the start of the First World War the firm of J.W. Singer at Frome, which was noted around the world for its iron work, church ornaments and statues, was requisitioned by the government to make munitions. Singer's wanted more space, so took over the market hall, close to its factory. This was turned into a foundry for making shell cases and fuses. Between July 1915 and December 1918 J.W. Singer made 1.6 million shell cases and more than 71.5 million cartridge cases. But it could be a dangerous way to earn a living. Records show that in 1917 a woman lost all the fingers of her right hand while cutting brass bars at a circular saw. The following year another woman suffered a severed finger. At the time the firm was employing a record 700 people and for the first time in its sixty-six-year history women were on its payroll.

The Ministry of Supply built a Royal Ordnance Factory at Bridgwater in the early days of the Second World War. It was built on a site between the villages of Puriton and Woolavington and designed to produce an experimental high explosive known as RDX. The factory was eventually privatised and later acquired by BAE Systems. It was closed in 2008 with the loss of 130 jobs.

War Office contracts for gloves for military pilots in the First World War meant that many men in Yeovil were exempt from serving in the armed forces. A Military Service Tribunal in 1917 heard that the many glove manufacturers in the town had large contracts from the government. The tribunal was told that it was vital that orders for gloves were met and completed by the end of the year by men who had experience of the industry. The tribunal decided to allow ninety-six of the ninety-nine applicants to stay in the factories until at least 1 February 1918. The cases of just three men were rejected.

Just before the outbreak of the Second World War, Pittards, one of the Yeovil firms in the gloving industry, started to produce what became known as 'Pilots' leather for gloves for the RAF. As a result the firm became a protected industry during the war years.

During the war years Westland Aircraft at Yeovil produced military aircraft including the Lysander, the Whirlwind and the Welkin.

The curtain came down at Weston-super-Mare's Knightstone Theatre during the early years of the Second World War when the building was taken over to become a factory making battledress.

WAR ROUND-UP

War Artist

Artist and graphic designer Alfred Leete (1867–1954), who attended Weston School of Art (now Weston College), designed the iconic First World War army recruiting poster with the slogan 'Your Country Needs You'. Leete's poster depicted Lord Kitchener, the British Secretary of State for War, wearing the cap of a British field marshal, staring and pointing at the viewer, calling them to enlist in the British Army against the Central Powers. Alfred Leete's family ran the Addington Hotel at Madeira Cove, Weston-super-Mare.

Bombs over Yeovil

Eighteen soldiers were killed in October and November 1940 in Yeovil during air raids by German aircraft. At Houndstone Camp five men lost their lives and at the neighbouring Lufton Camp the death toll was thirteen. All the soldiers were buried in the town cemetery in Preston Road

During the war Yeovil suffered enemy air raids on ten occasions; 107 high-explosive bombs fell on the town killing or fatally wounding forty-nine people. A further thirty-two were seriously injured and ninety slightly. Sixty-eight houses were totally destroyed, 2,377 were damaged but repairable, 309 had windows broken, and 67 were damaged by machine-gun fire – a total of repairable buildings of 2,753 – accounting for a third of the borough's houses. Fire bombs, however, did not fall on the town.

Prisoner-of-War Camps

Many country houses across the county were used as prisoner-of-war camps in both the world wars. They included an eighteenth-century family mansion built at the foot of the Quantock Hills and known as Sandhill Park. From 1914 onwards the mansion, which stood in its own parkland, accommodated German and Austrian officers.

After the war Somerset County Council converted the house into a home for handicapped children. However, Sandhill Park was requisitioned by the military again in 1940 and became a hospital, providing accommodation in tents and huts. Sandhill Park was eventually sold for housing development.

Eighteenth-century Barwick House, Yeovil, was variously used as a prisoner of war camp and an American army base.

Stoberry Park, Wells, housed Italian prisoners of war who were captured in the Western Desert campaigns.

College Take-Over

Fifteenth-century Butcombe Court in North Somerset, now divided into flats, became a school in 1942 when pupils from Clifton College Preparatory School, Bristol, moved in. They left their normal classrooms when soldiers from the American army took over various college buildings while they made arrangements for the D-Day Landings in 1944.

Dwight D. Eisenhower, the Supreme Allied Commander Europe, visited American troops camped in Weston-super-Mare in the build-up to D-Day. Rather than enjoy the comfort of a hotel, Eisenhower stayed overnight in a military caravan in Weston woods.

Home Town Visits

HMS *Burnham* was a First World War destroyer leased to Britain by the USA in the dark days of 1940 for vital convoy escort. It crossed the Atlantic no fewer than sixty-eight times.

HMS *Burnham* was adopted by Burnham-on-Sea. Crewmen who served on the destroyer visited the resort, which they called their 'home town', every Easter from 1981 to 2002. A plaque fixed to the wall of the Esplanade recalls the bond 'between ship and town'.

Digging for Victory

In both world wars golf courses were often used as allotments. Portishead golf course in north Somerset was a typical example, not onlywere vegetables grown there, but the clubhouse, which incorporated a windmill, was used by the Home Guard as their local base. The Dig for Victory campaign was set up by the British Ministry of Agriculture. People across the country were encouraged to grow their own food in times of harsh rationing.

Pier Taken Over

Birnbeck Pier in Weston-super-Mare was taken over by the Admiralty during the Second World War and became known as HMS *Birnbeck*. The pier was used for the development of secret weapons.

'Over and Out'

Portishead Radio, with its call sign GKA, played a vital role during the Second World War. It provided worldwide maritime and long-range aeronautical communications from 1928 until 2000, becoming the world's largest and busiest radiotelephony station. In 1974, for example, the station employed 154 radio operators who handled more than 20 million words a year. With the advancement of satellite communications the number of messages started to dwindle and the station closed in 2000 after more than seventy years in service. Portishead Radio's control centre was based at Highbridge, near Burnham-on-Sea. Its main transmitting station, which was remotely operated, originally consisted of a large array of radio masts at Portishead Down. It was later replaced by a single radio mast at Clevedon, which was in use until 1972.

15

SPORT

HOWZAT!

Somerset County Cricket Club was formed in 1875 after a two-day match between the Gentlemen of Somerset and the Gentlemen of Devon. It was played at Sidmouth, Devon, with Somerset winning by eight wickets. Somerset County Cricket Club made its first-class debut against Lancashire at Old Trafford in 1882.

The club is one of eighteen first-class county clubs that play each other in the county championship. Somerset has never won the title, its highest finish being second, which was achieved in 2001, 2010, 2012 and 2016.

However, the club's trophy cabinet is not bare. Somerset won its first silverware in the late 1970s, winning both the Gillette Cup and the John Player League in 1979. In the years since, the club has experienced some success in one-day cricket, winning the Gillette Cup on two further occasions, the Benson & Hedges Cup twice and the John Player League once more. The team has reached the final of the Twenty20 cup competition on four occasions.

In 1947 the club recorded the lowest ever score by a county cricket club when it was bowled out for 25 by Gloucestershire.

Somerset County Cricket Club has had its headquarters in

Taunton since 1882. Its ground has a capacity of 8,500. In 2006 it also became the home of England women's cricket team.

SOME NOTABLE SOMERSET CRICKETERS

Jack White (1891–1961) was something of a West Country cricketing legend. He played for Somerset from 1909 to 1937, taking 100 wickets a season fourteen times. In 1929 and 1930 White, from Holford, west Somerset, scored more than 1,000 runs, completing the 'cricketer's double'. In 1929 he was chosen by the cricketer's bible, the *Wisden Cricketers' Almanack*, as cricketer of the year. During his career with Somerset he scored 12,202 runs. He captained Somerset in 1927 to 1931 and also played in fifteen Test matches. White captained England in four of them.

Harold Gimblett, who came from farming stock at Bicknoller, made his debut for the club in 1935 at the age of 20. Gimblett, who was also selected to play for England, had a twenty-year career with Somerset. The cricket writer and Somerset historian David Foot described Harold Gimblett as 'the greatest batsman Somerset has ever produced' in a book about the player that was published in 1982.

Gimblett scored at a fast rate throughout his career, and hit 265 sixes. He left first-class cricket abruptly, suffering from mental health problems that would remain with him to the end of his life. Gimblett died in 1978 aged 64.

Bill Alley, an Australian, joined Somerset in 1957 and played in 350 first-class games for the club, the last one at the age of 49. In one season he scored more than 3,000 runs. He went on to play twelve seasons for Somerset, passing 1,000 runs ten times, scoring twenty-four centuries, including a double century at Nuneaton. In all the left-handed batsmen knocked up a total of 16,644 runs for the county. When he retired from first-class cricket, Alley became an umpire for sixteen years, standing in ten Test matches. Besides playing for Somerset, Alley turned out for other major teams including Commonwealth XI and New

South Wales. He died in Taunton aged 85.

In the 1970s three world-class cricketers, Viv Richards and Joel Garner, both from the West Indies, along with Ian Botham, transformed Somerset County Cricket Club. For the first time in the club's long history, the Somerset team became trophy winners. They won the Gillette Cup and the Sunday League in 1979. Then they went on to win the Benson & Hedges Cup in 1981 and 1982, and the NatWest Trophy in 1983. Garner, a fast bowler, was known as Big Bird on account of his height of 6ft 8in.

In 1986 Somerset Cricket Club was torn apart after the then team captain, Peter Roebuck, decided not to renew the contracts of Garner and Richards. Botham, who was close to both West Indian players, was unhappy about this decision and walked out on Somerset for good.

Botham is arguably one of the best-known personalities to have ever been associated with the county club. He was educated at Buckler's Mead comprehensive school in Yeovil and played for the county club 1974–87. He was captain from 1983 to 1985. Botham played in 102 Test matches for England, twelve as captain. After retiring from first-class cricket in 1993 he made marathon charity walks from John o' Groats to Land's End and across the Alps to raise money for leukaemia research.

WOMEN CRICKETERS

Anya Shrubsole from Bath made history by becoming the first woman to appear on the front cover of the *Wisden Cricketers' Almanack* in 2018. It marked England's World Cup win on home soil in the previous year. Shrubsole hit the winning runs in a tense semi-final victory against South Africa before her six for 46, which included five wickets in nineteen balls, brought England back from the brink of defeat as they edged out India in the Lord's final. A photo of Shrubsole holding the World Cup trophy appears on the traditional yellow jacket of the 155th edition of the *Almanack*, which has been published every year since 1864. Shrubsole, who has been a member of the England women's cricket team since 2008, was brought up playing boys' cricket at Bath Cricket Club. At the age of 13 she became the first girl to join the Somerset Academy. She now plays for Somerset Women's Cricket Club.

GOALS GALORE

Yeovil Town is the football club known as the 'giant killers'. The team is also well known for playing on a sloping pitch for many years. As a non-league club, Yeovil had a reputation for beating major Football League sides, especially in the FA Cup. One of the biggest surprises that filled the sports pages of national papers came in 1949, when Yeovil beat Sunderland 2-1 in the fourth round of the Cup. The visitors from the north-east were known as the Bank of England club on account of their strong financial backing. The attendance figure at Yeovil's Huish Park for that match was an all-time record of 17,123. Yeovil went on to play at Manchester United in the fifth round but lost 8-0 in front of more than 81,000 spectators.

Some of the 'Giant-Killers' Victories
During various FA Cup campaigns Yeovil Town has beaten many bigger clubs, including Hereford United (2-1) in a second round replay in December 1992; Fulham (1-0) in November 1993; Northampton (2-0) in November 1998; and a 1-0 victory over Blackpool in December 2000.

Following Yeovil's Progress

Although the club was founded in 1895, it took Yeovil Town, who play in green and white, 108 years to get into the Football League, when they were promoted from the Football Conference as champions in 2003. Yeovil Town were League Two champions in 2005 and League One play-off winners in 2013.

That Sloping Pitch!

Yeovil Town's original home was the Pen Mill Athletic Ground, next to the railway station. The club moved out in 1920 to Huish Park, which was notable for its pitch with its 8ft sideline-to-sideline slope. In 1990 Yeovil built a new stadium on the former Houndstone army camp, although the club still calls it Huish Park.

The Glovers

Most football clubs have nicknames, which usually derive from local history or a historic event. Yeovil Town is no exception. Its nickname is The Glovers – a reference to the history of glove-making in Yeovil, which was at its peak during the eighteenth and nineteenth centuries.

Some Yeovil Town FC Records

Most overall appearances: Len Harris, 691 (1958–72)

Most goals scored by a player: Johnny Hayward, 548 (1906–28)

Record attendance for a Football League match at HuishPark: 9,527 versus Leeds United, 25 April 2008 (Football League One)

Longest-serving player: Len Harris, fourteen years (1958–72)

Longest-serving manager: Billy Kingdon, eight years (1938–46)

Biggest victory in the Football League: 6-1 v Oxford United, 16 September 2004

Heaviest defeat in the Football League: 0-6 v Stevenage, 14 April 2012, 2-8 v Luton Town, 5 August 2017.

SOMERSET OLYMPIANS

Lizzie Yarnold became a double Olympic world champion in the 2018 Winter Olympics in South Korea, winning a second gold medal to go with the other she won four years earlier. The bob skeleton champion, who trains at Bath University, held on to her crown from the Sochi Olympics with a dramatic last run of the event to get into the record books. The 29-year-old is now Britain's most decorated Winter Olympian, with gold medals in two successive competitions. Yarnold calls her sled Mervyn, after a former work colleague who sponsored her when she needed money to continue competing. Yarnold was also chosen as the Great Britain flag bearer at the opening ceremony of the 2018 winter games.

Dom Parsons won Great Britain's first medal of the 2018 Winter Olympics with bronze in the men's skeleton. Parsons, aged 30, who is studying a PhD at Bath University, is Britain's first men's medallist in the event since John Crammond in 1948. Parsons finished tenth in the Winter Olympics at Sochi in 2014.

Former chalet maid Jenny Jones, who learnt to ski on the dry ski slope in Churchill when it was offering free lessons, became the first Briton to win an Olympic medal in a snow event. Jones collected a bronze medal in slope-style in the 2014 Winter Olympics in Sochi.

When Mary Bignal broke the womens' long jump record in the Summer Olympics at Tokyo in 1964 her local independent television station not only told its viewers of the news but installed a more permanent reminder of her success in her home town of Wells. Television Wales and West marked out the length Bignal had jumped – 22ft 2.25in. – on a brass strip, which is embedded in the pavement of Market Place. Bignal, who was educated at Millfield School, won a gold medal for her jump. She now lives in America and was the first British female athlete to win an Olympic gold medal in track and field.

Millfield School at Street has been represented at every Olympic Games since 1956, and at the 2012 Olympics in London, Millfield was the most represented school in Britain. Over the years Millfield has produced many rugby stars, including J.P.R. Williams (British Lions and Wales), Olly Morgan (Gloucester and England) and Mat Perry (British Lions and England).

HORSE POWER

Being on a main London-to-West Country route, Wincanton was an important staging town in the late eighteenth century. The coaching inns had stabling for 300 horses. The town's connection with horses is now mainly through Wincanton race course. It's believed the course staged the first ever National Hunt steeple chase in 1867. The racecourse, owned by the Jockey Club, now stages seventeen meetings between October and May of the following year. In the 1960s, Wincanton was taken over by Racecourse Holdings Trust, which owns fourteen other racecourses across the country.

IN THE SWIM

Crowds of people flocked to the seafront at Weston-super-Mare on the morning of 5 September 1927 to see Kathleen Thomas make some sporting history. The 21-year-old became the first person to swim the Bristol Channel between Wales and England. She set off from Penarth and the crossing to Weston took her seven hours and twenty minutes. Although the distance is 11 miles, it's actually calculated to be 22.5 once the brutal currents are factored in. Plenty of men had tried and failed to swim across the channel before Thomas's successful attempt.

The first person to use the new marine lake at Burnham-on-Sea in 1931 was the First Lord of the Admiralty, the Rt Hon. Albert Alexander, who was born in nearby Weston-super-

Mare. He ceremoniously rowed across the lake as part of the official opening event. The lake and swimming pool fell into disuse during the Second World War and was finally demolished in 1987.

PEDAL POWER

Dozens of elite cyclists pedalled into Weston-super-Mare in 1962 for the Tour of Britain Milk Race, so-called because from 1958 for thirty-five years the event was sponsored by the Milk Marketing Board. On Saturday, 8 June the cyclists arrived on the seafront at Weston-super-Mare having completed stage six of the tour, a gruelling 151 miles. On the following day the cyclists left the resort on the next stage, 138 miles to Northampton. The 1962 tour was won by Eugen Pokorny of Poland.

SCHOOL GAME

The Downside Ball Game is an outdoor racquet sport that has been played by pupils at Downside Abbey at Stratton-on-the-Fosse since 1820. Although it bears some similarities to the game of Fives, it is played with a solid wooden bat rather than one's hand. Four players – two on each side – take part.

FORE!

The golfer Harry Vardon, six times winner of the British Open and also a winner of the US Open, was commissioned in 1905 to design a golf course for the growing resort of Portishead. He produced plans for an eighteen-hole course on 83 acres of land at Nore Road, running alongside the Bristol Channel. Two dozen unemployed men were taken on to build the course. It was officially opened in July 1907 when Harry Vardon and J.H. Taylor, another British Open winner, staged an exhibition match.